Mountains, Rainbows and an Occasional Moose

Ammye,
My prayer is that my book will bless you.
Love,
Aunt Clyta

Clyta Coder

ISBN 978-1-64458-786-7 (paperback)
ISBN 978-1-64458-787-4 (digital)

Copyright © 2019 by Clyta Coder

All rights reserved. No part of this publication may be reproduced, distributed, or transmitted in any form or by any means, including photocopying, recording, or other electronic or mechanical methods without the prior written permission of the publisher. For permission requests, solicit the publisher via the address below.

Christian Faith Publishing, Inc.
832 Park Avenue
Meadville, PA 16335
www.christianfaithpublishing.com

Moose drawing by Antonio Wray Garcia

Printed in the United States of America

In memory of Frank W. Coder
and in honor of daughters
Ruth Coder Garcia and Jeanne Coder
and all the wonderful
friends we made in Alaska

Contents

Acknowledgements..7
Preface...9
Chapter 1:   Heading North..11
Chapter 2:   Cheechakos..24
Chapter 3:   Joy and Grief...38
Chapter 4:   Babies, Tomatoes, and Transmissions............43
Chapter 5:   Fairbanks, The Golden Heart City.................50
Chapter 6:   A Special Breed...62
Chapter 7:   The Writing Life...69
Chapter 8:   I'll Fly Away, Oh Glory.................................75
Chapter 9:   Hellos and Goodbyes....................................81
Chapter 10: Uncertain Days...89
Chapter 11: That's What Friends Are For..........................96
Chapter 12: Fairbanks Farewell..127
Chapter 13: Moving On..132
Chapter 14: Stormy Weather..141
Chapter 15: Summer in Cordova......................................150
Chapter 16: New in Town—Again....................................158
Chapter 17: Holidays in Glennallen..................................169
Chapter 18: The Inside Story...175
Chapter 19: On the Road Again.......................................186
Chapter 20: A Winding Road...196
Chapter 21: Kansas City and Beyond...............................203
Chapter 22: One Day at a Time.......................................207
Chapter 23: Facing Future..218

Acknowledgements

I would like to thank Alice Sudlow with The Write Practice who offered editorial comments. I would also like to thank Janice Clayton and Lauree Wilkerson who read the manuscript and offered help with grammar and continuity.

And special thanks to my grandson Antonio Wray Garcia who created the moose drawing.

PREFACE

In retrospect, I did not feel free, until recently, to share a part of my life that in many ways shaped who I am today. The seven years that my husband, Frank Coder, and I lived in Alaska were full of highs and lows—the fondest dreams yet the deepest disappointments. Now, I write to share my love for that far land I lived in: the faith that the ups and downs tempered in me, the dark of December, the all-night-sun days of June. I write of my faith journey to help others who might be traveling through valleys of doubt and discouragement.

To speak of our life in Alaska was difficult for Frank, and in the remaining years of his life, he was silent; but my daughters were born there, and I want to tell them of its beauty and of the friends who influenced our lives. I want my daughters to know and understand their father better as he was then, full of hopes and dreams. I want to share with them and my family and friends the fun times and the laughter. For those who wonder what it would be like to live in Alaska, I want to share my experiences.

And, I join with the apostle Paul, for I write of what I now know in part in the promise that someday I will know fully and be fully known.

Chapter 1

Heading North

Go from your country...to the land that I will show you.
—*Genesis 12:1 (NRSV)*

Smoke rose from the chimney of the rustic log cabin roadhouse in Tok, Alaska, inviting us to rest after our long day's drive. Crisp, cool air refreshed our weary bodies. The acrid smell of wood burning perfumed the air.

"I could murder a steak or a couple of burgers," Frank said.

"Me too. I'm starving."

Inside, an attractive young waitress smoothed her auburn hair and mustard-splattered apron. She walked toward us order pad in hand and gave us a wary look, like a mouse chased by a cat.

"Hello, folks, how are you this evening?" Before we could answer, the young woman continued, "Please forgive our limited menu tonight, but it's been two weeks since a supply truck's come. You can have roast beef sandwiches or hamburgers, without onion, tomato, cheese or fries. We don't have milk because our last delivery arrived spoiled." She threw up her hands. "I'm so sorry."

The poor girl looked close to tears, and I had to quell the urge to pat her on the shoulder and say, "That's okay, honey."

Instead, Frank replied with a smile, "Don't worry about it. We'll have two roast beef sandwiches and chips, if you have 'em." Hungry and exhausted—no time for us to be picky.

With a relieved look, she walked to the kitchen.

Enter two men dressed in brown hunting jackets and caps and reeking of stale tobacco. They waited patiently for about three minutes, left in a huff, returned ten minutes later. "They ain't no other place in town open," the older man complained.

Sighing, the waitress approached them and repeated the reduced menu.

"I'll have the deluxe hamburger," the younger man said with a wink.

"Deluxe? Well, that will be without lettuce, tomatoes, or cheese and no fries, but we have potato chips."

He frowned. "How about a stack of hotcakes?"

"No milk, eggs, or flour."

The older man grinned and asked in a gravelly voice, "If I bring in a moose steak, will you fix it?"

"Sorry. That's against health department rules."

"Four hamburgers then."

The waitress noted this and asked, "You want four bags of chips to go with 'em?"

Everyone laughed at the lighthearted banter. Friendly camaraderie in an isolated roadhouse welcomed us, Frank and Clyta Coder, to Alaska where we soon learned that late supply deliveries are a fact of life.

*****

Our journey to Alaska began in Salinas, California. Frank had graduated from Southwestern Seminary, Fort Worth, Texas in December 1973 with a master of church music. He accepted a position as minister of music and youth at a church in Salinas.

From the beginning, there was friction. The pastor often disliked Frank's choice of hymns. Frank liked the liturgical hymns of Charles Wesley, although he appreciated and was willing to incorporate the more personal gospel hymns too. The pastor had a beautiful voice, and if he wanted to sing or wanted his son to lead choruses, it didn't matter what the choir had rehearsed, the pastor would have his way. This became a problem, and because their goals were too different, Frank resigned after eleven months.

Difficult days followed his resignation. In January, 1975, I suffered the third miscarriage in eight years. When we arrived home from the clinic, I prayed, "Lord, why can't I carry a child to birth? What's wrong with me?" Bitter tears flowed from my broken heart.

Frank pulled me to him. "The stress of the last several months probably contributed." His voice broke, and we grieved together.

No new job opportunities came Frank's way that winter, and he decided to enroll in an education course at San Jose State to pursue a teaching certificate. He wanted to teach music in either elementary or secondary and be a part-time choir director in a church. He remained open to full-time ministry and sent out several resumes.

One response was particularly intriguing. A small Baptist church in Kenai (Key-nigh), Alaska, a town 158 miles southwest of Anchorage, needed a minister of music and youth. He decided to apply.

Thoughts like the following marched through my head: *A crazy idea—Alaska. It's three thousand miles away, and isn't it frozen most of the year?* In 1972, while living in Fort Worth, Texas, I had read an article about a couple in Anchorage and wondered what it would be like to live there. At the time, I thought, *Naw, we will never do that*, but never say never. In fact, had I known what we faced in the ministry, I would have crawled under the bed in our apartment at seminary and stayed there.

Many factors came into play. Our sadness over the loss of the baby and the anxiety caused by Frank's unemployment convinced us we needed a change. We were mission volunteers, and the denominational board liked to appoint missionaries who were no more than thirty-two years of age. Frank was thirty-two and I thirty-one. Because we were up against the age limit, our appointment appeared less likely. However, we both agreed that Alaska certainly qualified as a mission field because of its isolation small congregations, fewer churches, and fewer people who wanted to minister in them. We already had experience working in small congregations in California, and the work challenged us. In addition, we loved the rugged terrain of wilderness areas and liked the idea of camping and exploring the Pacific Northwest.

A coworker piqued my curiosity. "Alaska is a land of snow-capped mountains and midnight sun," she said. Her father had owned a bookstore in Anchorage. Still, fears threatened to overcome my excitement and enthusiasm. Alaska was a long way from the continental United States. If things did not work out, what then?

Frank brought home books, brochures, whatever he could find, and we became excited about the prospects of a ministry there. One evening, he sat down in the living room and picked up an article on Alaska. Staring at it, he said, "The unknowns of a move to Alaska are about as large as the mountains pictured here."

"Yes," I agreed, "we'd be leaving family and friends and moving a long way on limited funds."

"Are we running away from an uncomfortable situation here, or does the Lord have a place for us up north?"

"Our ministry during college and seminary taught us an important kernel of truth."

"What do you mean?" Frank asked.

"Whether we are in Texas, California, or Alaska, we have to work with people, flesh and blood Christians from all walks of life."

We sat in silence for a while, and in the days following, prayed, asking that if God wanted us in Kenai, the church would extend a call. Slowly, a calm assurance motivated us to pursue this new ministry.

Frank sent a letter of introduction to the Kenai church and asked for more information about the position. Pastor Bob Bedwell replied, "The church was established in the early sixties. We have a membership of around one hundred. Many of our members work on the offshore oil platforms in Cook Inlet and for Conoco Phillips. The position would require you to supplement your income with substitute teaching or some other part-time employment."

He handed me the letter. I read it, and we listened to the taped sermon the pastor had sent.

"What do you think?" Frank asked.

"In his sermon, he said faith is acting as if something is so that's not so, so it can become so. I like that definition of faith." I smiled. "He did use a lot of so's, though."

Frank chuckled. "Yes, the sermon is pretty good. I'm going to ask some definite questions about the type of music they sing in worship and what they feel are the responsibilities of a youth minister."

Frank received letters from the pastor and the chairman of the deacons. They all agreed that the youth ministry was their first priority and liked his idea of developing the ministry through the Sunday school and a youth council. The pastor said Frank would be given freedom to choose the hymns and music. He said that he was not a singer himself and would never insist that an individual or group sing if Frank had other plans. His only suggestion was that Frank use a variety of music to lead not only the youth but the entire congregation in worship.

We left the unknowns in God's hands, and several weeks later, the church voted to offer Frank the position of music and youth minister. After more prayer and discussion, we accepted the call.

*****

Now the time had come to prepare for the long journey.

Frank understood engines and car parts and could maintain a vehicle and avoid expensive repairs. This would be especially important not only on the long and rough roads to Alaska, but also while living there. In addition to his automotive expertise, he liked working with wood and could use saws and hand tools of all kinds.

We drove a 1971 standard transmission Ford Maverick, and with it we would pull a homemade trailer approximately six feet long, four feet wide, and four feet high. When we bought the trailer in Riverside, California in 1971, it had been an old camping trailer that Frank stripped down to the bed and rebuilt with aluminum sides, wooden back, top, and doors. The trailer had carried all our belongings to Texas and back to California and would now carry our furnishings to Alaska.

We loaded a bed, a couch, a homemade wooden desk with removable legs, household furnishings, stereo components, tent, and camping gear into the trailer and covered everything with heavy plastic in case the trailer leaked. Our large collection of record albums and books were mailed to the Kenai church.

*****

We dreaded telling our families that we were moving to Alaska.

Frank called his father in Arkansas. In his gruff voice, Mr. Coder said, "There's not enough churches in the United States? You have to go to another country?" He'd apparently missed Alaska's admission to the Union in 1959.

How could I explain it to Grandmother? She was getting older and, for the last ten years every time we left Tulsa, had said, "Well, honey, you may never see me again."

On the first page of a letter to her, I emphasized the importance of obeying God and explained we had answered the call to serve a church in another state. "The church," I wrote on the next page, "is in Kenai, Alaska, near Anchorage."

Grandmother immediately wrote back, "Clyta, why can't Frank take a church in Oklahoma or Arkansas?"

Writing to Mother was easier. She always considered what her children did as their business and only said, "If that's what you think you should do, honey, you have my blessings, but we'll miss you".

Likewise, Frank's mother and stepfather in California simply wished us well.

Determined to answer the call of the north, we assured them of our love and thanked them for their concern.

*****

On Sunday morning, August 31, 1975 we left Salinas for Kenai, Alaska, a distance of over 3,000 miles. The prospect of traveling 1,100 miles on gravel roads in Canada, through British Columbia, and the Yukon failed to daunt our enthusiasm. We had prayed, asking God to give us a safe journey each day, and we trusted Him to do it.

We drove the first 478 miles and stopped that evening in Grants Pass, Oregon. The verdant pine-covered mountains and rocky coastline of the Pacific Northwest took our minds off fears of the unknown. Youth and adventure pumped in our veins.

Monday evening found us in Bellingham, Washington, where Frank purchased heavy- duty tires the next morning. We checked route information in *The Milepost,* a travel guide so named because locations along the Alaska Highway are designated by mileposts. This invaluable resource included detailed maps with the distances between gas stations—information that could be a lifesaver. It showed alternate routes to help novice travelers determine whether their vehicle could handle road conditions or if a route might save time or offer unusual scenery. *The Milepost* also described towns and villages, lodging, campgrounds, places to buy food and supplies.

Photographs of the towering mountains and flowing rivers of British Columbia increased our enthusiasm. However, the Canadian border guard forced us back to reality by asking, "How much money are you carrying for your trip through Canada?"

"Seven hundred dollars," Frank replied and assured him that the church would wire us more if needed. A white lie—we trusted they would. In truth, we had more faith than money.

He stared at us for a long moment, rubber-stamped our entry permit, then flashed a friendly smile.

"Be careful and you'll be okay."

Our first impression of British Columbians, or BC'ers, rang true in every encounter with them: refreshingly friendly and helpful.

From the border, we followed the West Access Route through verdant pasturelands that housed dairy farms with high-roofed red barns. Blue-eyed Marys, orange globe mallows, and reddish-brown vine maples sprinkled the meadows. The highway followed the rushing Fraser River bordered by proud pined-mountains that sloped down to meet it. We struggled with the desire to view and photograph the scenery versus the need to make time. Near Cache Creek, we drove through flatter terrain. Large ponds and lakes reflected trees and sky like a glass surface painting.

After 281 miles of hard driving that day, we were tired when we reached the Lac La Hache campground about six o'clock and pitched our tent.

A man approached us. "Hi, folks, why don't you come and share our campfire."

"Thanks," Frank said. He glanced at the stick the man waved in the air.

"Don't worry, the stick is for roasting marshmallows," the man replied and turned to his friend. "Bud, where are they?"

"Forgot them at the last stop, remember."

Happy to share something with our campmates, I said, "You can have some of ours." We soon learned Dave and his friend Bud were Californians, going to Alaska to do some fishing. The good-natured men kept us laughing with their stories until it was time to turn in.

We enjoyed tent camping. However, camping in Canada and Alaska has an added element. Hint: They are large, furry, and can be black or brown. Every sound became grunts or scratching. Sleep eluded me and Frank had a sick stomach all night, nerves I think. We rose early Tuesday morning to a golden sunrise and continued our journey "oohing" and "aahing" at such splendor.

This ended abruptly when we hit a rough shoulder and ran off the road. *Great. Not even on gravel yet and already in trouble.* We thanked God that the car and trailer remained upright, but the trauma played tricks on my mind.

"Lost the keychain Mother gave me. Pictures of bluebonnets… loved it," I mumbled through sobs, frantically searching the roadside without spotting it.

Frank hugged me and said, "Look, we're not hurt. We didn't lose our lives, only a keychain."

Within minutes four men approached in a truck.

"Havin' a bit of trouble, eh?" one man said. "We'll have you out in a jiffy." They pulled our car out of the ditch, refused to accept payment, and called a wrecker to tow us to a garage. The mechanic's bill, a mere fifteen dollars to tighten the trailer hitch, convinced us further of the generous spirit of BC'ers.

Back on the road, lucky us we saw a black bear running across the road near Chetwynd, our day's destination. Many travelers never get to see wildlife up close.

Thursday morning, our journey took us from Chetwynd, toward Fort St. John. We had driven approximately 1,500 miles, about halfway to Kenai, Alaska. Instead of going through Dawson Creek, we chose to cut off a few miles by taking the more scenic route through Hudson Hope. Autumn had painted amber gold and purple hues on the hillsides. Morning fog lent a mystic air. The tiny village nestled in hills overlooking the Peace River was once a fur-trading post and later the head of navigations for steamboats.

"Beautiful country," the clerk agreed when we stopped at a small grocery, "but the isolation in winter can be lonely,"

How isolated would Kenai be? I wondered.

Putting aside these doubts, we prepared to leave the pavement at mile 93 for 1,100 miles of gravel road. First Frank had to install the handy-dandy bug screen and headlight protector. The directions assured us the package contained all the needed parts. It did, with a few leftover!

"Install the protector on the grill of the car in an upright position," I read.

That sounded simple enough. However, thirty minutes into the project, Frank scratched his head and said, "I may sue the manufacturer."

A car approached from the opposite direction, its grill slimy with bug carcasses. The driver rolled down his window.

"Having problems? The headlight covers are all you need. There won't be many bugs."

His grill proved otherwise, and I opened my mouth to point that out. Frank gave me a look and replied, "Thanks, we're fine." He turned to me and added, "I paid $18.34 for this screen, and by golly, I'm going to use it."

When he finished the installation after much fussing and fuming, I commented, "The contraption must be called a bug screen because installing it drives you buggy."

"Har, har, very funny. Mosquitoes are what's causing the buggy sensation."

We had forgotten to douse ourselves with insect repellent before getting out of the car. Canada and Alaska are a swarm of mosquitoes from snow melt to snow fall. Scratching and griping, we vowed to spray next time.

*****

Near Fort St. John, we forgot our itches while we listened to the everyday happenings on Caribou Radio.

"Now for this morning's job opportunities"—loud crash—"apparently this morning's job opportunities are not available."

One program broadcasted messages to remote areas. We laughed at "Please return my dentures. I need them. Call Horsefly 582."

Boredom—not an option on the highway. A rock traveling at an estimated speed of one hundred miles per hour cracked our windshield. In those days, no one traveled the Al-Can without losing a windshield. About three minutes later, we hit five enormous potholes, one right after the other. The combination of jolting on the gravel road and the earlier off-road jaunt caused my body to ache and did not improve my whiplash, the result of an auto accident the year before.

A few miles beyond Fort St. John, we drove by Pink Mountain, so named because the red-barked willows lend a pink hue to the mountain when bathed in the sunlight of a fall morning. White spruce, poplar, and aspen bordered the highway approaching the town of Fort Nelson. Named for the British admiral Lord Horatio Nelson, it is surrounded by the Muskwa, Fort Nelson, and Prophet Rivers.

By Friday, we headed west from Fort Nelson. The highway crisscrossed rivers and streams and was bordered by densely forested land. We meandered upward through the Canadian Rockies with scenic vistas such as Steamboat Mountain summit. At Milepost 392, we came to Summit Pass, elevation 4,250 feet, the highest summit on the Alaska Highway, where we pulled off the road a moment to photograph the scene and reflect on its beauty.

"Wow! Look at those rocky crevices already powdered with snow," Frank said.

"So beautiful," I whispered, wanting to savor the majestic silence. I wished my mind's eye were a camera lens to capture each panorama of God's majestic creation.

Alas, we had to journey on. The weather changes rapidly in this area, and soon the rains caught us. Frequent downpours coupled with road construction caused a slippery mess and repeated delays. Cars passed us and sloshed mud on any part of the car that wasn't already dirty.

Later that day, the rain stopped and the sun peeked through. Frank drove into a shallow creek to wash off the mud.

"You missed a spot," I yelled, supervising from a distance.

"Oh, yeah," he replied. "Here." He formed his hands into a shovel and bailed water at me.

*****

Near Whitehorse, about ten o'clock in the evening, we watched a spectacular sunset—purple and crimson clouds cast a rosy glow over the mountains. On the radio, Glen Campbell sang, "Rhinestone Cowboy" for the umpteenth time. Anytime I hear that song, I am back on the Alaska Highway.

Intensified bumps and grinds punctured our euphoria due to the rough roads. Thankful to see the lights of Whitehorse in the distance, we found a lovely campsite.

"Oh, thank you, Lord. It has a laundry and hot showers," I said. Only those who camp for several days can fully appreciate how welcome a hot shower can be—steamy water caressed our bodies, washed away grime and cares, and soothed sore muscles. Temperatures hung around forty degrees Fahrenheit. The attendant built a campfire, and we slept warm. Our twenty-dollar tent proved trustworthy.

Saturday morning dawned cold and misty. We dismissed the idea of reviving the campfire and breakfasted in Whitehorse at a rustic café with reasonably priced man-sized helpings of fried eggs and Canadian bacon. The clientele ranged from long-haired teens in jeans to gnarly bearded old-timers.

One gray-beard seated across from us asked, "Where do you folks hail from?"

"California, and we're headed to Alaska," I answered.

"Ain't everybody." He flashed a toothless grin, inviting more conversation.

"How did Whitehorse get its name?" Frank said.

"Well, early miners chose the name 'cause the foaming rapids looked like the manes of white horses. The town was built about 1900 and was the northern end of the White Pass and Yukon railway. Most of the people of Yukon Territory live in Whitehorse."

Bidding our friend goodbye, we photographed the three-story log cabin "skyscraper" and the famous old log church while waiting for the Bank of Montreal to open. Had we not wanted to be in Kenai by Sunday, further exploration of the historic city would have been fun. As it was, larger rocks, enormous potholes, and three sections of roadwork caused more delays. However, driving difficulties were a small price to pay for the privilege of seeing the glacier peaks of the mountain range surrounding Lake Kluane. After Kluane, we drove through the snowcapped Elias Mountains. Autumn gold met snow white as the sun came out to warm us.

"Wow. I wonder if Alaska could be more beautiful than Canada?" I said, smiling at Frank.

"We'll soon find out."

After we ate dinner at the roadhouse in Tok Saturday night, exhausted, we headed straight to bed. Sunday morning found us up early anticipating our arrival in Kenai that evening after eight days of hard driving. It was time to emerge from an adventurous road trip to the responsibilities of a new job in a harsh climate—the reality of being there.

I believe driving three thousand miles from California was the perfect way for us to meet Alaska. We got a condensed view of life on the last frontier—the long daylight hours of late summer, the spectacular scenery, the sparse population. Also, we experienced firsthand the community spirit and helpfulness of north country people.

And we experienced a lot of mud. Our car was a hog that had wallowed in a mud hole getting a snout full of dead bugs. Since every other car looked the same, it made us feel right at home.

Chapter 2

Cheechakos

By faith he stayed for a time in the land...
—*Hebrews 11:9*

I want to buy a car that a moose can't push off the road.
—*Kenai resident*

On Sunday we traveled on the Tok Cutoff toward Gakona where we would catch the Richardson Highway for a short fourteen miles to Glennallen. Our seven-day journey to Kenai was coming to a close. Trees lined the highway—paper birch, balsam, and black-and-white spruce. The terrain changed to wetlands along Lower Station Creek.

"The Milepost says to watch for swans on the pond we're approaching," I said.

"Swans? Are you sure?'

"Yes. It says 80 percent of the world's trumpeter swans nest in Alaska. The smaller tundra swans have a bright yellow mark on their black bills."

Not one of them showed themselves to us that day. This taught us an important lesson: Wildlife follow their own schedule, not ours. We hoped for better luck next time.

The road climbed to six thousand feet, and from Mentasta Summit we viewed an array of marshmallow-topped peaks that stretched into the horizon. Later we drove through the small town of Glennallen where we listened to "Glorious Things of Thee are Spoken" on the local radio station. I noticed Frank's eyes mist with tears and covered his hand with mine.

"Haydn's music touched my soul," he whispered.

"I understand." Often a classical composition evoked an emotional response in him like nothing else could.

We reflected on the beauty of music and mountains for the next twenty-five miles to Eureka Summit Lodge. The lodge was located on the Glenn Highway between Mount Sanford to the east, the Talkeeetna Mountains to the west, and the Chugach Mountains to the south. A tasty stew warmed and relaxed us while we looked at attractive photos of Dall sheep and caribou, trophy salmon, and moose that adorned the walls of the large dining area. Dressed in flannel shirts, vests and hunting caps, the clientele laughed and talked like old friends. I longed to be one of them and hoped to find such camaraderie in our new home.

We determined to drive the 275 miles to Kenai and arrive that evening. Daylight was in our favor because even in September, the sun would not set until nine o'clock in the evening.

Anchorage surprised us with traffic lights and cars bumper-to-bumper.

"Let's see, we're at Northern Lights Boulevard and Seward Highway. Look, Frank," I said.

"Sears is often the first retail store to arrive. Didn't expect traffic lights, though."

The city sprawled with a population of a little over one hundred thousand, largely due to the influx of oil pipeline construction employees. Distant mountains surrounded the meandering roads and highways. I always thought of Anchorage as a small city in the wilderness and, indeed, residents of the Kenai Peninsula and Southcentral Alaska referred to it as the city.

From Anchorage, we headed south on the Seward Highway along Cook Inlet. The inlet covers 180 miles from the Gulf of Alaska to Anchorage, and branches into the Knik Arm. The highway follows the north shore of Turnagain Arm with its panoramic view of the south shore and the Kenai Mountains.

"Knik must be a Native American word, but Turnagain Arm—what a crazy name."

I checked the travel guide for an explanation and learned that Captain Cook discovered that neither the Placer nor the Matanuska river led to the northwest. His superior, Captain Bligh, named the inlet Turnagain Arm because the exploration party had to turn around.

"It's too late for us to turn around," Frank said. "We have found Alaska."

A rainbow appeared over Turnagain Arm to welcome us. It inspired me to write this poem:

> *Amber gold along the Alaskan road*
> *speaks to the autumn in our hearts,*
> *shades of emotion blend together, form*
> *lives ready to shed leaves of the past*
> *and be washed clean in an Alaskan winter.*
> *Rich, deep colors of promise—a*
> *rainbow over Turnagain Arm.*

Along this fifty-two-mile stretch of the Seward Highway were vistas of the Chugach and Kenai mountain ranges interspersed with small cascading waterfalls. A brochure had described beluga whales frolicking in the inlet and noted that belugas are white and not hard to identify. I peered through the binoculars.

"See anything?" Frank asked.

"Maybe—a large white shape way out there." My heart beat faster. A whale would be something to write home about. However, the white mass disappeared, and though I searched a while longer, it never reappeared.

I aimed the binoculars up the rock wall on the east side of the highway and caught a huge Dall sheep in the crosshairs, a majestic creature. The big guy wore a handsome two-horned crown and gave me an imperious stare as if to say, "Driving, huh? Bet *you* can't climb up here."

According to the Alaska Department of Fish and Game, a male Dall sheep, or ram, can grow up to three hundred pounds and can be found in the subarctic mountain ranges of Alaska. At three years, rams have massive curled horns and are easily recognized. They flee to the rocks and crags when danger approaches.

The sheep perched on the rocky precipice brought to mind the biblical promise in Psalm 18:32–33: *"God girded me with strength and made my way safe. He made my feet like the feet of a deer, and set me secure on the heights."*

We would need God's strength in our new work.

Kenai

At Soldotna, we took the Kenai Spur Road the last ten miles. The town of Kenai was spread out along the highway and had a small shopping center, a gas station, and convenience store. Frank telephoned the pastor from the gas station.

"Pastor, Frank Coder. We're finally here. So sorry we didn't make it for the Sunday night service, but we can't drive fast with this trailer." After he had talked a few more minutes, he added, "Thanks for understanding."

"The pastor said he would meet us at the church. It's right on the highway, and we can't miss it."

Somehow we did miss it—drove past, back and spotted it. The tan wooden church building was set near the Kenai bluff, surrounded by tall pine trees and made me think of "The Little Brown Church in the Vale."

A man got out of his car and walked toward us, his plaid flannel shirt, waterproof jacket, and blue jeans stretched tight across his short stocky frame.

"Bob Bedwell," he said, reaching out to shake hands. "Welcome to our liquid sunshine." Bob still had the twang he brought from Texas. In fact, I had never heard of anyone refer to "my-rads" of angels, and it took me a while to work out he meant myriads when I heard him preach the first Sunday.

"Great to be here," Frank said.

"Bet you're tired. Ima Jean made sandwiches and baked brownies. She and the kids are anxious to meet you."

We followed him about a quarter mile to the parsonage. Red-haired Jeannette, the eleven-year-old, and her younger sister, Gina, five years or so, ran outside, grinning.

"Hi," they chorused before shyness claimed them and they retreated behind their mother where ten-year old David stood.

Ima smiled and said, "You're here safe and sound. Come on in and eat while there are still some brownies left." She gave Bob and the kids a knowing look. Bob led us through a wooden enclosure before we reached the front door.

He noticed my puzzled expression and said, "This is an arctic entryway. It keeps the frigid air from rushing into the house. Some people just hang a blanket in front of the door. You'll be cheechakos for a while," Bob teased.

Cheechakos, or newcomer, originated in Chinook jargon, and also meant someone who has not yet lived through an Alaska winter.

Their friendliness cheered us. We chatted around the dining room table and shared experiences of the highway, thankful for the yummy food. After dinner, I helped Ima Jean put away the rest of the groceries they had recently purchased in Anchorage.

Looking at a box labeled Milkman, I asked "Powdered milk?"

"Yes. We buy a couple of gallons of fresh milk when we go to Anchorage, about every six weeks, and when it's gone, we use this. Not bad if you refrigerate it until cold before you drink it."

During the grocery put-up, yawns overcame me, though I tried to suppress them.

"Listen, we've driven the highway ourselves. You must be exhausted so let me show you to your room."

Frank went right to sleep. I lay awake for a while, nagged by questions. Would the congregation accept us? Would they like Frank's style of leadership?

A restless sleep finally claimed me, filled with dreams of falling, falling, unable to stop, a forever dream. When I awoke with a shudder, 2:00 a.m. showed on the clock face. My overtired mind magnified the obstacles we might encounter until they grew distorted like images in a carnival mirror. Not wanting to disturb Frank, I lulled myself back to sleep.

"You were exhausted," Frank replied Monday morning when I told him about my dream. He held me for a moment. "I have qualms too, but let's try to be positive."

Ima Jean dropped the kids off at school after breakfast and went to her job at a local bank. She was a lovely person, and I soon learned what a supportive wife and caring mother she was.

Bob took us to find an apartment and gave us a tour of the town.

"Kenai has a population of around five thousand. Many of them—and a lot of men at church—work for Tesoro on oil drilling platforms in Cook Inlet or they work for Conoco Phillips," Bob explained.

The town had grown since pre-oil pipeline days. In addition to the post office and gas station, the shopping center had a Northern Commercial store. Grocery prices at the small store were sky-high. Everyone told us that the money we would save by driving to Anchorage to buy groceries and needed supplies in quantity would pay for the cost of the trip. I made grocery lists from a running list of needs and daily menus. If we ran out of something, we paid the higher local price or did without.

We rented a modern two-bedroom apartment close to town overlooking the bluff. That evening, we stood in front of our apartment and, with the aid of binoculars, watched beluga whales frolic offshore against the background of Mount Redoubt climbing majestically skyward, already dusted with snow. The sun painted a mural of gold and magenta as it sank into the bay.

"Makes moving to Alaska worth all the effort, doesn't it?" Frank said. He put his arm around my shoulder.

"Wow!" I said, not finding sufficient words to express my awe. We had begun to fall under the spell of this beautiful land.

Frank painted his office at the church bright purple and chartreuse, colors he thought the young people might enjoy. The adults were a little taken aback, but the teenagers loved it and soon began to congregate there. Church members greeted us with friendliness and acceptance the next Sunday and presented us with a pounding—a generous donation of food and basic needs to help a family set up housekeeping. We were most grateful.

*****

In addition to his employment at the church, Frank began to substitute teach to supplement our income. I visited the local employment office seeking a clerk-typist position and landed a job in a most unusual way. The employment counselor suggested the Kenai Medical Clinic as a possible employer. I passed the typing test, and she scheduled an interview for me with Dr. Peter O. Hansen who needed a medical transcriptionist.

The doctor was a tall slender man, fortyish, quiet, and businesslike. He explained the requirements of the position. The typist must straighten the waiting room, water a large rather bedraggled-looking plant, and vacuum every room each day. Dr. Hansen referred to Pastor Bob as Reverend Birdwell, and I didn't correct him. He asked me a few questions about myself and, to my surprise, offered me a job on the spot.

"The job sounds interesting and a good way to get to know the community and local people." I paused. "Could I have a day to think it over?"

"Yes, though I'd like to make a decision in the next couple of days."

On Thursday evening, Frank had a meeting with the youth council. Bed sounded good to me, but before I reached it, the doorbell rang. Pastor Bob and Dr. Hansen greeted me.

"Surprise," Bob said. "I had more groceries to deliver, and Dr. Hansen called and wanted to talk to you."

"Please come in, how about something to drink?"

Both declined, and not one for small talk, Dr. Hansen said, "I'd like for you to come to work for me."

Wow—what an unusual home visit from a doctor. For a few minutes I didn't know how to answer then decided what the heck and forged ahead.

"About the job, since you also expect housekeeping duties, would you consider increasing the hourly wage?" I held my breath. *Did I say that?*

He hesitated a moment, offered me a dollar more, and I accepted. (I don't remember the exact amount, but Alaska minimum wage in 1975 was $2.10.) The clerk at the employment office chuckled and said, "The doctor must have had a change of heart to offer you more money."

Friendly and helpful, the clinic staff included Aaron, the physician's assistant; Gail, the bookkeeper; Abby, the receptionist; and two nurses, Deidre and Nancy. Dr. Hansen decided to switch me to the position of receptionist because he liked the way I related to the patients.

The doc proved to be a fair, if somewhat eccentric, employer. No dust must be left on any surface, including the waxy leaves of the plant, and he usually found any missed speck on the carpet. The plant must not be too moist or too dry. Karolee, his wife, sometimes served as his nurse. She disapproved of the waiting room reading material, in particular, risqué pictures in the *Cosmopolitan* magazine.

One afternoon, after a particularly trying morning when his wife had encouraged him to rid the office of "those magazines," he peeked around the corner and spied a female patient who, he claimed, flirted with anything in pants. Under his breath he muttered, "Not her and *Cosmo* too." A rescheduled appointment put him in a better mood, and Karolee convinced him to remove *Cosmo* from the waiting room.

Each day brought a new challenge for me. One icy morning, Dr. Hansen met me in the hallway.

"Clyta, I need you to go to the post office to get the mail and to the bank to make a deposit. Here's the keys to my truck." With no further explanation, he went into an examination room.

"I've never driven a truck, let alone on ice," I said to Gail. She gave me a sympathetic look and shrugged.

I picked up the phone and called Frank. "Couldn't you take me? You know I've never driven a truck."

"No. Just do it. I'm sure he has insurance." Frank knew I had to get used to driving in ice and snow.

The good doctor forgot to warn me about the steep incline on the street that approached the post office. I slid through the intersection and landed safely about ten feet from the front door. What a relief to be in one piece, with no dents on the truck, when I arrived back at the clinic.

Moose Mania

Each summer, Doctor Hansen hired a fourth-year medical student to intern. Dr. Mike, a New Yorker, had been at the clinic since June. In spite of driving all over the peninsula peering through binoculars, he had not seen even one moose, Dall sheep, or bear. The bookkeeper nudged Mike toward the door one day when returned from lunch.

"Get out there. A moose and calf are running down Main Street."

He soon returned looking gloomy. By the time he got outside, the moose were gone. Viewing wildlife wasn't in the cards for Mike. Moose abound in Alaska, though not necessarily where visitors can view them. He left without seeing even a ptarmigan, a bird commonly seen in the area.

Better that, though, then the encounter one man had with a giant bull moose. Pastor Bob told us about a conversation he overheard at a local café.

"I'm going to Anchorage to buy a truck that a moose can't push off the road," a man complained. "Sunday night on the Kenai Spur road a bull moose appeared out of nowhere. I stepped on the brake and the durn thing pushed my VW bug onto the shoulder. Luckily, I lay on the horn, and he bolted."

MOUNTAINS, RAINBOWS AND AN OCCASIONAL MOOSE

The Alaska moose is a strange-looking creature. Standing five or six feet tall, awkwardly proportioned, with bulbous facial features and kind of a vacant expression. For me, the moose symbolized the many differences between life in Alaska and anywhere else we had lived.

Learning to speak Alaskan took some doing. The first Sunday at church, a young woman told me, "I haven't been outside for three years." I gave her a startled look. She had infant twins and a five-year-old, but she couldn't be that housebound.

She noticed my confusion and explained, "You know, to California. We say *outside or the lower forty-eight* for anywhere in the continental United States.

"Oh, of course. Can you tell me, though, doesn't *sourdough* mean an old-timer? You call your kids sourdoughs."

"Yes, because they were born in Alaska. The term describes anyone who has survived at least one winter, too."

My vocabulary soon expanded, and I began to pepper conversations with colloquial expressions: when the *snow flies* for first snowfall and *breakup* for the melting of snow and ice each spring.

One Saturday, a couple invited us to their homestead. After bouncing over a rutted road for about a mile, we approached what looked like the foundation of a house with a chimney and a roof.

"Come on in," Sharon greeted us. She led us down the concrete steps to the door. We drank a mug of coffee and chatted for a few minutes before the men went out back to see something Robert was building.

Sharon sighed. "We built this *daylight basement* with a temporary roof and weather proofing two summers ago before the snow flew. Last summer a trip to Missouri and the short construction season slowed us down. This summer, rain interfered. We're still in the basement with no time to finish it this year."

"Well, maybe next summer," I said.

"Maybe." She looked doubtful. "The problem is, Robert loves to hunt and fish, and Alaska summers usually offer ample opportunity for both."

I don't know if they ever finished the house.

Everyday Life

In addition to Alaskan lingo, we had to learn to drive safely in snow and ice and to maintain a car in subzero temperatures. Studded snow tires were a necessity, and a driver needed to change to oil that could handle the cold. People learned to keep their vehicles in good mechanical condition and carry extra warm clothing, a sleeping bag, cans of Sterno and matches to use for heat in case of a breakdown.

An engine block heater also needed to be installed. This was a small electric device attached to the engine. It needed to be plugged in for couple of hours when the temperatures dipped below twenty degrees. Outlets for this could usually be found outside most buildings and homes. However, it took a car about two hours to cool down after it had been running, so if the car were to be driven within two hours, there was no need to plug it in.

We also had to dress for cold weather. Temperatures in coastal Alaska were milder than in the interior. They rarely went below minus twenty degrees. On our first winter in Kenai, the thermometer hovered between zero and twenty degrees above zero, as though the weather wanted to give us a gradual orientation.

On the first day, the temperatures dipped to forty degrees I walked the two blocks to work because Frank needed the car. Dressing in layers was important—proper clothing prevented frostbite and could save your life; however, I went slightly overboard. Under a heavy sweater, I wore a flannel shirt and thermal underwear. On top of all that, a heavy coat, woolen scarf, and stocking cap. All these clothes caused me to move like a mummy.

Deidre watched me unlayer and began to laugh.

"Whew," I said. "Thought it would be colder."

"Last year it barely got below zero here, and a sweater plus a heavy jacket was adequate. If it gets colder than that, a goose down parka with a fur-lined hood, wool cap, gloves, and insulated boots are what you need."

As our choice of clothing adjusted to temperature, our eating habits adjusted to available foods. Frank never liked powdered milk, but I drank it if it was cold. We ate fresh fruit and vegetables while they lasted and depended on frozen and canned foods after that.

"Fresh fruit and lettuce are expensive. Next summer you can pick cranberries, blueberries, and raspberries for vitamin C and fiber," Aaron, the PA at the clinic, told me.

"Right now, you could still pick some rose hips. They're abundant from August and till the snow flies," Gail, the receptionist, added. "They are the fruit of wild roses and are rich in vitamin C. The small pink petals have a mild sweet taste when brewed for tea, and the berries can be made into jelly and catsup."

The University of Alaska Cooperative Extension Service had free brochures to guide the novice berry picker. And for a dollar, I purchased a copy of *Wild Edible and Poisonous Plants of Alaska* and kept it close at hand. Research told us that rose hips are also rich in iron, calcium, and vitamins A, B, and E.

Summer and fall found people fishing for salmon, Dolly Varden trout, and halibut or digging clams. In season, most hunted moose, and the church was on the road-kill list or names of nonprofits the highway department called when a moose was hit by a car or truck. The drawback to this was that when called, a person had to get the moose any time of day or night, skin it, and process it to avoid spoilage.

Frank was neither a fisherman nor a hunter, but our congregation kept us supplied with canned salmon and moose meat. Moose cuts taste like beef, and most cooks soak them in milk overnight and use meat tenderizer. The meat can be cut in thin strips and fried in oil or used in chili or stew.

Kenai had a movie theatre, but TV reception was terrible, and programs were tape delayed. One Sunday morning the Sunday school superintendent missed Sunday school and didn't appear to rehearse his bass solo for the choir anthem.

At eleven o'clock, Frank walked to the choir room for something he'd forgotten just as John walked in. "We were getting worried. Did you have car trouble?" he asked.

"Sorry I'm late. We…uh…well, something came up."

He found his place in the choir, with no further explanation. John was forever a Texan and a football fan. In private, he told Frank, "A tape delayed Cowboys game aired this morning, and I wanted to watch it and figured Sunday school could go on without me. Sorry I wasn't here to rehearse."

Frank stared at him in disbelief and the other choir members were less than enthusiastic.

The above scenario describes television in Kenai. As for radio reception, the local station only transmitted during daylight hours and played pop, country, and Western music. Frank had to rely on his personal record collection for classical music. Mostly we made our own fun by visiting with friends to share stories, sing, or play dominoes or cards.

You might say that oil built Kenai's Olympic-sized pool since most residents were employed in some capacity by oil companies. Outdoor fun included downhill and cross-country skiing, ice skating, riding on snow machines, and watching local sled dog races.

*****

In November, the pastor's wife and I flew to Anchorage after work to join our husbands who were at a church conference. Everyone assured me Wien Air Alaska had a reputation for safety. The outside of the plane had impressed me with a huge picture of a native Alaskan in a fur parka. It began snowing lightly just before liftoff.

"Ima Jan," I said, "is it my imagination, or do I see snow through the tiny gap between the frame and the door."

She laughed. "You see snow. At least it isn't blowing in on us." Observing my look of alarm, she added, "Don't worry, Alaska Airlines has a reputation for landing safely."

Shivering, I pulled my heavy coat closer. We landed without incident, and it was the first of my many flights with the man in the fur parka.

While in Anchorage, we stayed with one of the local church members in their lovely log cabin home. Huge windows afforded a gorgeous view of the distant mountains. We relaxed with cups of hot chocolate in front of a blazing fire.

Christmas approached, and with it came our first heavy snowfall. Looking out the apartment window toward the old Russian Orthodox church and the bluff, we watched huge flakes flutter down and turn the peninsula into an icy wonderland.

We opened the gifts sent by our families in Oklahoma, Arkansas and California and telephoned them, which brought them closer. I still have the woolen scarf my mother sent me that year. In Alaska, where most people are a long way from home, friends become family too. Celebration of Christmas and New Years with the Bedwells turned our thoughts to what 1976 might bring.

Chapter 3

Joy and Grief

> *Weeping may linger for the night but joy comes with the morning.*
> —Psalm 30:5b

We greeted the New Year with enthusiasm for the music and youth ministry at the church. Our biggest excitement had nothing to do with Alaska, not directly anyway. My father-in-law later credited the long winter nights. In November, Dr. Hansen had confirmed that after almost ten years of marriage, I was indeed pregnant. Our first baby would be born in July.

Though the doctor said he understood how much we wanted to tell everyone, he suggested that we wait three months. I had suffered three miscarriages, all in the first trimester, and the doctor urged caution. Between November and January, I lived somewhere between walking on eggshells and floating on a cloud. Now we could share the news.

"Dad, you're finally gonna be a grandpa," my husband shouted into the phone.

For nine years, Mr. Coder had constantly asked when we planned to have children.

"Elsie! Frank and Clyta are gonna have a baby in July," Mr. Coder yelled. Then to Frank, "We're happy for you, son. But you can't have a baby in that frozen wilderness. Why don't you move back here?"

This was an old song because Mr. Coder couldn't understand why anyone would not choose to live in Arkansas. My mom knew how much we wanted a baby and rejoiced with us. Frank's mother and stepfather were happy for us too.

Grandmother wrote her congratulations and added a sad note—my grandfather's arteriosclerosis weakened him and caused him to be confused much of the time In February, I wrote her this letter:

> My prayers are with you and Papa. I know it's hard on you seeing him ill and feeling helpless. I'm thankful you have many loved ones there to help and comfort you. Not being able to be there physically is hard for me, but in praying for you, sometimes I feel so close to each of you and so close to God that His presence and yours fill the room. Christ's bond of love is truly a gift to each of us.
>
> Tell Papa how much we love him and are praying for him.

Here is a poem I wrote when I lost the baby last year:

> *"We have also a more sure word of prophecy...as unto a light that shines in a dark place, until the day dawn, and the day star arise in your hearts"* (2 Peter 1:19).
>
> In deep darkness of despair
> In night's dark place when no one's there,
> You are, Lord—a lamp shining.
>
> Your word of prophecy is sure,
> Your kindnesses endure
> You are, my Lord—the day dawning.
>
> When hand grips hand in fear,
> When the pit seems very near
> You are Christ—the Morning Star appearing.

Papa died March 25, 1976, and Doctor Hansen felt it would be dangerous for me to fly home. A mixture of sorrow and guilt made for a heavy heart. The day of the funeral, I was with caring women at a prayer retreat. They held my hands, shared my grief, and prayed for me—helping me through this difficult time.

*****

With each month, parenthood grew from a hope to a probability. We kept busy in spite of the short days—only six hours of daylight between November and the end of January. The eighteen hours of darkness never really bothered me because I worked inside and life went on about the same. Like many people, my husband found it slightly depressing. Dueling church members didn't help.

One Wednesday night, after prayer meeting, Frank came home looking glum. I had stayed home with a cold.

"What's wrong?" I asked.

"A committee met with me tonight and said many are disappointed in my leadership. I'm not bringing enough new people into the church to justify my pay. Some think I don't relate well to the congregation. Others want to sing more familiar hymns and choruses. They might ask me to resign."

Stunned, I muttered, "Six months, and they are making a decision like that? Now, when we're expecting a baby?"

During the next few weeks, Frank met with various groups and individuals in the church. It seemed the congregation was split on the issue. One evening, the pastor came by.

"I could have handled the disagreements in the church better," he said. "Everyone liked our summer youth director. He had a magnetic personality that drew young people to him. You're quieter and more reserved. People began complaining. I listened to them instead of praying and talking with you about it."

Frank's reply will always remain with me. He pointed out the positive things he had done and the people he knew he had helped, and with tears in his eyes, he said, "I don't know what's going to happen, but I'm claiming the verse in Job that says, 'Though He slay me, yet will I trust Him' Job 13:15 (KJV)."

An older pastor in the Brethren church took Frank under his wing, listened when he needed to talk, and encouraged him to persevere. Several of the women took me to shop for patterns and material to make maternity clothes—a pair of pants and top and a skirt and blouse—all interchangeable. Many assured us of their support for Frank's ministry. When the church voted to ask us to stay, we breathed a sigh of relief.

Kenai Peninsula Messiah Chorus

Meanwhile, Frank had formed a community chorus to perform the Easter portion of Handel's *Messiah*. He sent notices to the peninsula communities—Soldotna, Seward and Homer—and received an encouraging response.

Musicians in Alaska are always eager for opportunities to perform. Thirteen area churches agreed to participate. The volunteer musicians included seven soloists, forty-five choristers, four pianists, and a small orchestra of four violinists, one cellist, a bassoonist, two trumpeters, and a timpanist. Frank directed the vocal and instrumental ensemble each week in the choral room at Kenai Junior High School.

Messiah is not the most difficult classical composition to perform, though it is not easy either. Some had sung the music two or three times, some had never sung it.

At the first rehearsal, Frank told the group why he felt *Messiah* is one of the most meaningful sacred compositions ever written.

"George Frederick Handel composed music to share Christ's story of redemption. Librettist Charles Jennens compiled the scripture text. We are singing the Easter portion of *Messiah* and will sing arias based on the following scriptures, John 1:29 and Isaiah 53:3–6, plus many others. You might recognize the text in aria titles such as 'Behold the Lamb of God,' 'Surely He Hath Born Our Griefs,' and 'I Know that my Redeemer Liveth.'"

Frank told how Handel completed the composition in twenty-four days and that *Messiah* was a turning point in the composer's life.

"My prayer is that each of you will be blessed by singing God's word set to music. I pray that our performance on Easter Sunday will bring to life the message of God's love."

Our choir and orchestra persevered and worked hard. Harsh winter weather and road conditions proved our greatest obstacle, especially for Karen Hornaday, the cellist, who drove over one hundred miles from Homer for the last four weekly rehearsals. Luckily for us, the Kenai Peninsula experienced one of the mildest winters in years.

As performance day neared, we wondered if we would be able to pull it off. Our brave director spent hours on technique. With the musical score in front of him, he played and conducted a recording of the Philadelphia Orchestra and the Mormon Tabernacle Choir.

To our relief, Easter morning, April 18, dawned clear and cold without new snowfall as had been predicted. At three o'clock that afternoon, around five hundred people gathered in the Junior High school gymnasium to hear the Kenai Peninsula *Messiah* Chorus and Orchestra. We sang and played with gusto and received a standing ovation—a glorious Hallelujah.

The performance, a success beyond our highest hopes, highlighted our first year in Alaska.

CHAPTER 4

Babies, Tomatoes, and Transmissions

> *For everything there is a season...a time to be born...a time to plant.*
> —*Ecclesiastes 3:1a–2a*

With the stress of the *Messiah* performance over, it was time to plan for the baby. One morning, I pulled Frank into the room that we planned to make into a nursery.

"We'll put the crib against the inside wall where it will be warmer. What do you think?"

Frank stared out the window. I sensed his mind was not on baby furniture. "You're right," he said, facing me. "That's the best place for the crib." He paused. "And this east facing window will be perfect for growing tomatoes in a window box. I have directions for building one and—"

"Frank Coder, we're having a baby, not a bumper crop of tomatoes."

He rambled on. "In Alaska, you have to grow tomatoes inside."

"That may be, but—"

"The baby will be clear across the room from the tomatoes. I don't understand all the fuss," he responded. Because he often came up with creative solutions that somehow worked, I tried to see his point. We could be more self-sufficient.

When I described Frank's plan to Dr. Hansen, my obstetrician and boss, he chuckled. "Often expectant women go into the nesting mode and determine to redecorate the house. I've never heard of a prospective father wanting to plant a garden in the nursery. Be patient. He'll probably give up the idea."

Doc knew best. Frank built a window box in the dining room and planted his tomatoes.

*****

A few weeks after the tomato episode, he decided the transmission in our '71 Maverick needed to be replaced. It was worn out after moving us from California to Texas, back to California, and three thousand miles to Alaska, each time pulling our homemade trailer filled with everything we owned.

Armed with a Chilton repair manual, he and a friend went to Anchorage and returned with a transmission kit and bucket seats.

"I'll have to replace the bench seat because the new gearshift has to go on the floor," he explained. "What's more, to fit the Maverick, the gear shift must be installed backwards."

"Backwards?" I croaked.

"Backwards. Reverse will be at the upper far right, then down to first, over and up to second, down to third, ending with fourth in the upper left-hand corner. You see?"

What I saw was me struggling to shift in that pattern without stripping the gears or burning out the clutch. My affair with stick shift and clutch was rocky and probably had something to do with our need for a new transmission. But I was seven months pregnant and didn't feel like debating. Frank had often saved us a bundle by repairing our vehicles. I decided to trust his judgment.

He diagrammed the *H* shifting pattern and made me study it. Like Professor Harold Hill in *The Music Man,* Frank believed in the "think system." I cannot explain how my brain reprogrammed my hands and feet to shift in a reverse pattern. Truthfully, I don't believe it was much more difficult than when I first learned to drive a car with a standard transmission. To do that, I had to master coordination of brake, gas pedal, and clutch with the gear shift. Somehow reversing the procedure came to me easier than learning to drive a stick shift in the first place.

Because my mother did not own a car, I didn't learn to drive until after I married. Frank tried for three years to teach me on our standard Studebaker. Each driving lesson ended with me in tears. We bought a Toyota with an automatic transmission in 1969, and I learned to drive it.

The Toyota turned out to be a lemon, and in May of 1971, without discussing it with me, Frank traded it in on a Ford with a standard transmission. The next day, he once more showed me how to shift and use the clutch, made me drive him to work and drive back home, lurching all the way. Four hours later, I had to return to his work place to get him.

We lived on a busy divided highway in West Riverside, California. I will never forget the horror of seeing a policeman immediately behind me as I faced a U-turn up an incline. Attempting to coordinate gas with clutch, I prayed, took several deep breaths, and gunned it, not daring to glance back at the officer. I was relieved when no siren or flashing lights followed. How much harder could it be to learn to shift in reverse?

Our tomato vines yielded an abundant crop in August— and by then, I also mastered the revised shifting pattern of the Maverick.

*****

People often ask me what was different about having a baby "up there." In some ways, it was quite a bit the same as in any community in the lower forty-eight. We lived in a small town off a good highway, not in the bush country where no road goes and airplane or ferry are the only travel options. My doctor's clinic was nearby, and the well-equipped hospital in Soldotna where I would go was ten miles away.

The night before Ruthie was born, I checked into the hospital about five o'clock, Thursday evening, July 8. The sun never set that night—it kind of slid across the sky.

None of our family members were present due to the distance and cost of travel. Frank stayed with me the entire time, but I probably missed my mother more that night than at any other time in my life.

At nine o'clock, the pain became more intense. I threw my decision to have natural childbirth out the window, asked for a pain reliever, and the doc gave me a shot of Demerol. Big mistake. Contractions came to a halt, and he had to give me Pitocin to restart my engine. Sixteen hours later, at one o'clock in the afternoon, July 9, 1976, Ruth Michelle Coder was born.

Frank was the first one to hold her, and I'll never forget his bright smile as he turned to me and said, "It's a girl!" as if such a thing had never happened to anyone else. After wanting a baby for ten years, my heart overflowed with thankfulness that such a tiny perfect creature belonged to me. On the other hand, I was exhausted and content for the nurses to look after her while I slept.

Dr. Hansen was also with me through it all, and the office staff had to cancel his appointments that day.

The response of the community was typical of small-town America. Due to the *Messiah* Chorus and because of our church involvement, most of the women in town had called every five minutes during the labor to check on my progress. I overheard one nurse ask another "Who *is* she?" I'm sure they were glad when we went home Saturday night.

*****

Back at home, in order to keep the midnight sun out, we covered the windows with aluminum foil. This worked well, but we were still sleep deprived because Ruthie had colic. I remember Frank saying, "She has a powerful set of lungs. I could hear her the minute I drove into the parking lot."

Night blurred into day during the next six weeks. Thanks to the church women who had given me a shower in May, we had to buy almost nothing for the baby, not even a bed. I received plenty of house help and didn't have to cook a meal for two weeks or more. Our church family took good care of us, and though I appreciated the extra help, sometimes I longed for time to myself.

Two weeks after her birth, Frank and I celebrated our tenth wedding anniversary by going out to eat while a trusted friend kept the baby. What I remember most was my emotional high—delicious food and a new baby at home—a happy world. Ruthie slept the entire time we were out, but when we arrived home, refused to sleep for another six hours, exhausting her inexperienced mom and dad.

We needed reinforcements, and the second week in August my mother flew in from Oklahoma. Though my parents were married for twelve years, my father was an alcoholic and absent when each of us was born. Mom was small in stature and big in determination. She raised five daughters as a single mother.

When she entered the airport, Frank had walked away for a few moments, and she saw only me with the baby. Two years and many miles had come and gone since we had been together. We held each other and laughed and cried for several moments.

"You looked so alone," she said. "I saw myself all those years ago."

"Believe me, Mom, I have not been alone for ages it seems."

Mother fell in love with Ruthie and Alaska, in that order, and took charge for a few days to let me rest. "She's beautiful. I'm so happy for you."

We were not too tired to show her the land we had come to love. She ate halibut at Anchor Point in a café with a lovely view of the river. We paid an unbelievable five dollars for a meal of halibut and side dishes. Ruthie was not in the best mood that day, and Mom, Frank, and I took turns walking with her to prevent her disturbing other diners. Afterward, we continued on the Sterling Highway to Homer on the Southwest side of the Kenai Peninsula. The day was partly cloudy, but from East End Road we were able to view three glaciers, located on the far side of Kachemak Bay (the Russian name that means "high cliffs on the water"). They were majestic with their ice-covered peaks.

"God's creation surely smiled on Homer. It's breathtaking," Mother said.

On another day, she and I joined a friend who was a rock hound to look for agates on the beach. Agates are a banded form of finely grained quartz. Their color pattern and banding make them translucent, and each one is unique. Most of the ones my friend helped us find were rose and green.

A couple of days before Mother left, she and Frank went to pick wild blueberries. When they returned, I asked them if they felt the mild tremor.

"Now that ground-shaking experience was one I could have done without," Mother told me.

We said goodbye at the airport, and I wondered how long it would be before we saw each other again, but she had a life to get back to and so did we.

*****

In August, we sensed our days in Kenai were numbered. Rumbles and grumbles erupted from church members, but this time directed at the pastor. Pastor Bedwell had a good heart and loved the people. He had thought he could complete his seminary degree that summer. Though he was unable to arrange to take the coursework, he and his wife and children took a few weeks to visit family in the lower forty-eight. Some members did not understand this.

Bruce, the young man who had been a summer youth director the year before, came to preach in the pastor's absence. He did a good job, and the people liked him. In spite of this, church membership declined while the pastor was gone and didn't increase with his return.

Also, a faction of the congregation still did not accept Frank's ministry though he had assumed additional responsibilities in the absence of the pastor. Discouragement and frustration, combined with his new parental responsibility, led him to seek new opportunities.

A larger church in Fairbanks was the light at the end of the tunnel. The congregation flew us to Fairbanks for an interview. They were a friendly church, and we immediately liked Pastor Don Davis and his wife, Beth. He and Frank agreed on doctrine and music choice, and we felt good about the situation. The church extended a call for Frank to be their minister of music and youth. In October, with many tears, we bid goodbye to beautiful Kenai and all of our friends.

*****

Writer and artist Rockwell Kent, in his book *Wilderness,* summed up my feelings about the Kenai Peninsula.

> Ah, the evenings are beautiful here and the early mornings when the days are fair!... No sudden springing of the sun into the sky and out again at night; but so gradual, so circuitous a coming and a going that nearly the whole day is twilight and the quiet rose color of morning and evening seems almost to meet at noon. (24)

Chapter 5

Fairbanks, The Golden Heart City

For it is God who is at work in you, enabling you both to will and to work for His good pleasure.
—*Philippians 2:13*

Leaving Kenai

Kenai, in Southcentral Alaska, had been a good introduction to life in the north country. Its milder temperatures hovered around zero as compared to the minus twenty or thirty in the interior. Our bodies had a chance to become climatized. Now we prepared to move north and inland to a harsher climate in Fairbanks.

We filled our Kenai scrapbook with warm memories of new friends, the joy of welcoming our firstborn daughter and the success of the *Messiah* chorus. Our experiences were sometimes overwhelming, sometimes painful, and always an opportunity for growth.

We knew forming friendships in each congregation was an important part of a meaningful ministry because we had both grown up in the church and had been nurtured by church members. Also, we, like most Alaskans, were far from home. Church friends became family, and like any family, they wanted to wish us well.

Glenda Kenner gave us a copy of *The Layman's Parallel Bible* with her memorable inscription: *I will always remember the past year with loving memories.* Another friend, Jean, made us a unique baby quilt with fabric paintings of seals, Eskimos, and kayaks on each square. Church members also gave us a large cream-colored vase with a log cabin scene and a birch tree hand painted in black by Wasilla artist Ricky Gronewald. The vase remains one of my favorite possessions. We made time for farewell parties in between the usual preparations for a move.

*****

Packing, unpacking, and packing again had become a familiar routine. The day before we left Kenai, Pastor Don Davis and two deacons, Van Bowman and Ray Morgan, drove a truck from Fairbanks to Kenai, 516 miles. Frank worked with them to load our larger pieces of furniture into Van's truck. We enjoyed their good-natured ribbing. Don, a Texan, wore jeans and a plaid flannel shirt. He rattled off "Aggie" jokes one after another.

Frank had no Aggie jokes, but chimed in with, "Have you heard the one about the halo statue?"

"I don't think so, tell us," Don said.

"There was a man with a thick accent who hired a contractor to build a house and told him, 'I wan' a 'halo-statue' in every room.' The man went away on business, and when he returned to take a walk-through in his house, there was an arched alcove with a shelf on it built into a wall in each room. The man asked the builder, 'Why did you a-build theese shelves in every room?'

"Those are to put your halo statues on. You said you wanted one in every room."

"No, no, no, I wanna a thing in every room that goes a-*ring, ring* and you pick it up and say '*Ha-lo*', '*statch-you?*'"

Frank loved to tell that joke. He and his new audience laughed uproariously for several minutes. The relaxed attitude of these jovial men relieved some of his concerns over the move.

The "movers" left Tuesday morning. We followed a few hours later, pulling our homemade trailer with the rest of the furniture and household goods. Our first destination was Anchorage where we spent the night in a motel. Ruthie slept fitfully, waking often to interrupt our sleep. The next day, she slept the blissful sleep of an infant who doesn't have to worry about details like driving.

On Wednesday, we hit the Glenn Highway for the first 35 miles of our 358-mile drive to Fairbanks. Soon we turned onto the Parks Highway. In a sense, the Parks has a dual meaning—George Parks was the territorial governor from 1925–1933 and, it also is the most direct route to Mount McKinley Park (or Denali as it is now called). In early October, snow had not fallen on that section of highway, which made it easier to pull our homemade trailer.

Radio reception remained clear, and I remember hearing the lyrics, "Way down South in Birmingham, I mean South in Alabam…"

"We're sure far from Alabama," I commented.

"Or any other state," Frank said, "and moving farther north."

The road remained dry until we hit the mountainous area near Talkeetna and Mount McKinley National Park. Light snowfall rested on rugged peaks, settled into craggy boulders, and dusted tall pines and vegetation along the highway. The snow painted a pretty picture.

"I hope we can see at least a part of Mount McKinley," I said.

"Me too. Since we can't drive into the park today, just a glimpse would be nice. Right now, though, it's getting harder to drive, and I'm going to have to put on chains."

After a while, we drove out of the snow, and he stopped once more to remove the chains. A few miles further we ran into road construction. Frustrating, though we knew roads had to be maintained before winter settled in. We could not see McKinley that day and vowed to return one day to explore.

Thirty-six miles south of Cantwell, we traversed the Hurricane Gulch Bridge, a breathtaking 258 feet above the white water of Hurricane Creek and canyon. Crossing it did not scare me as long as I didn't look straight down.

To help us make time, I had packed sandwiches, cookies, and sodas, and we ate while driving.

"I wonder how different Fairbanks will be from Kenai," I said.

"You don't have long to wonder. We'll be there about five o'clock."

Welcome to Fairbanks

Beth Davis met us at the door when we arrived at our new home in Fairbanks.

"You must be exhausted," she said. "I brought homemade stew and cornbread." She apologized for the absence of her husband, Pastor Don, who had left on a trip outside to take care of family business. "Van and Ray set up your bed in the larger bedroom and the crib in one of the smaller ones," she said.

"Those are welcome words. Thank you," Frank said. "We sure appreciated their driving to Kenai to help us move."

"Van and Ray are great guys who are always there when you need them," Beth said. She was a petite blonde with a vivacious personality, smart, too, an accountant with the Internal Revenue Service.

"Van wants to show you the town Friday, after you've had a day to catch your breath."

"That would be a great help. Learning how to get around in a new town is always a challenge," I said.

"Especially for you." Frank winked at me.

"He's referring to the fact that I have no sense of direction and can get turned around in even the smallest of towns," I told Beth.

She laughed. "Well, Fairbanks is an easy town to learn."

When Beth left, Ruthie's cry reminded us she was hungry and so were we. After dinner, we looked around our new home. Frank's Uncle Bud had worked at Eilson Air Force Base in the 1960s and had joked that we'd probably have to live in an igloo. Not true. The house was a modern three-bedroom home in a residential area, off Airport Way. It had a nice backyard and up-to-date amenities, even a dishwasher and a washer and dryer. We counted our blessings.

Tour of Fairbanks

On Friday morning, Van Bowman came by for us. He was a tall handsome Kentuckian, friendly and outgoing. We drove a few blocks from our neighborhood and saw Alaskaland (now called Pioneer Park). The park was established in 1967 for the Alaska Centennial

Exposition, the one-hundred-year celebration of the purchase of Alaska from Russia.

"One of our church members owns an antique store in Alaskaland. Every summer, she flies to Tennessee to visit family and shop for antiques. She buys a truck, loads it with antiques, and drives it back to Fairbanks, sells the antiques in her shop, and sells the truck for enough to pay for the trip."

I laughed. "She probably has sold pieces purchased in Tennessee to tourists from Georgia, which they take back with them.

"I imagine so," said Van.

"Where's the University of Alaska?" Frank asked.

"That's where we're headed," Van answered in his pleasant Kentucky drawl.

The campus set on a hill covered with white spruce and birch trees. It sloped to a plateau to meet other small hills. In 1976, the campus consisted of three- or four two-story classroom buildings and two dormitories. The college focused on the sciences but offered a liberal arts degree and teaching certificates in all fields. Next, we drove to Fort Wainwright Army post.

"Don was stationed here after World War II," Van said. "That's how he and Beth got to Alaska. Several church members are stationed here. The men who hunt and fish love Alaska. Most of the women, though, don't like the cold and isolation. They complain and can't wait for their husbands to be transferred—kind of irritating to those of us who love this country."

Van drove downtown and turned on Barnette Street.

"Wasn't Fairbanks founded by a man with that name?" Frank asked, pointing to the street sign.

"Yeah, E.T. Barnette, kind of a shady character. In 1901, he came up the Chena River on a steamboat and settled here. Barnette exaggerated reports of the gold discovery of 1902, was even accused of salting a mine shaft with gold. Word spread about easy diggings, and by 1905, thousands of people had come to get rich."

"Looks like a lot of them stayed," I said.

We learned that the population of Fairbanks was about sixty thousand and that because residents found Fairbanks a friendly town, it was sometimes called the "Golden Heart" city.

"Van, how did you happen to come to Alaska?" Frank asked.

"I've been a salesman all my life. Started selling cars first and later went into auctioneering. When I heard about the proposed building of the Alaska pipeline, I knew people would come with it. I moved here to start the Fairbanks Auction Company. We made friends and liked the town so we stayed."

Later when we got out of the car to collect Ruthie, we thanked Van for the tour and added, "Fairbanks has a lot to offer, and we look forward to ministering here."

Getting Settled

Autumn daytime temperatures averaged forty degrees the first few weeks we lived in Fairbanks. I busied myself getting the house and yard in order and Frank made sure the car was properly winterized. We already had an engine block heater, but to this he added battery pad and oil pan heaters and a three-way cord with a lighted end to plug them all in. He also adjusted the engine coolant by adding minus-sixty-degree antifreeze. Kenai weather had been mild, and we needed to prepare for interior Alaska weather. Having a good auto mechanic for a husband was a blessing.

Frank also went right to work meeting with the pastor and church staff to set goals for the youth and music ministry. Don and he got along well right from the start. We looked for ways to get to know the church members.

One Saturday, Beth called. "Why don't you and Frank go with us to Van's auction today."

"Sure, we'd love to," I said. We had met Van's wife, Wanda, and sons Kai and Keith who worked with him in his business.

Beth told us how to get to the Trade Fair Centre on old Richardson Highway where the auction was to be held. We bundled Ruthie in her red fleece lined sleeper and a blanket, donned our heavy coats, and took off.

"There it is on the left. Van said it used to belong to the army," Frank said and pointed to a large Quonset hut. A Quonset hut is a prefabricated building set on steel trusses and built of a semicircular arched roof of corrugated metal insulated with wood fiber.

From the full parking lot, we could hear Van auctioneering. He had a strong low-pitched voice, was easy to listen to, and we discovered he knew how to work a crowd.

"Bid $5, $7.50, $10. I got $12 here, $15 over there. Do I hear $20? Sold your way number 22." Van's chant was understandable, though spoken at high speed, like an old 33-rpm record played at the speed of a 78.

Don and Beth greeted us, and I asked, "Why are Kai and Keith holding those numbers?

"They're ring men and select items for the auctioneer, holding them in view of the audience. Wanda is the clerk. She issues each bidder a numbered flash card and records name, address, phone, and driver's license numbers on the entry sheet. Bidders flash their numbers to make a bid," Beth explained.

"Frank, you and Clyta walk around and look at the items and we'll watch the baby," Don offered.

"You've got a deal," I said.

Frank found a wooden file cabinet and a chest of drawers, two things we needed, though we decided they could wait until a later day. Frank and I attended several auctions to see Van at work. and to people watch, a fun way to spend an afternoon.

*****

A new church staff member and his spouse feel much like students on the first day at a new school—nervous and overwhelmed. Caring congregants like Ethyl Peasgood, the church pianist, smoothed out some of the wrinkles.

Ethyl and Gloria Taylor, the church organist, liked Frank's plan to teach those interested, to play the recorder, a small wooden flute-like instrument. He had collected a set of alto and soprano recorders and arranged some simple music. A group met every Wednesday night before choir practice and soon were tootling away.

In small churches, like most in Alaska, staffing the church nursery was a thorny issue. We had a nursery worker for the Sunday services and sometimes Becky, the pastor's ten-year-old daughter, entertained Ruthie for me during Wednesday night choir practice. I often held her during prayer meeting, at the back of the sanctuary, and if she was still awake during choir practice, jiggled her up and down while I sang. It's no surprise to me that Ruthie began singing at an early age.

Our congregation kept us busy. Pastor Don suffered from a form of Lupus—a painful autoimmune disease that causes swelling, extreme joint, muscle, and chest pain—a major reason he needed an associate. One Wednesday evening, three weeks after our move to Fairbanks, I walked out of the church nursery and saw Pastor Don, red in the face, stumbling toward me clutching his chest and moaning.

"Don, what's wrong?" I asked, alarmed.

"Get Beth," he mumbled.

I immediately went for Beth who was in the recorder group and then ran for one of the deacons. Beth and a deacon took Don home and put him to bed, while Frank held the fort at church. A week in bed and Don felt well enough to resume responsibilities.

Frank tried to relieve some of the pastor's workload by visiting and helping edit the bulletin and church newsletter in addition to his other duties. For my part, I served alongside Frank, offered emotional and spiritual support, and tried to keep things running well at home. We formed a bond with Don and Beth, listened, and prayed with and for them.

Holidays

On our first Thanksgiving in Fairbanks, we joined several church members at Van and Wanda Bowman's beautiful home. Van provided the meat, and each of us brought our favorite Thanksgiving dish. We ate and ate, took a break to play dominoes, share stories, take naps, then returned to eat again. In '76, there were no in-home videos. Van rented the movie *The Pink Panther* and showed it on a projector—altogether a memorable day.

*****

Winter in Fairbanks meant shorter days—darkness and a full moon at three o'clock in the afternoon. The early darkness sometimes bothered Frank, but with a new baby, my days and nights often blended into each other anyway.

Snow flew in December that year in Fairbanks. Huge crystal flakes fluttered to the ground, making the world a marshmallow wonderland. Every time I witnessed a first snowfall, the beauty of it thrilled me. Snow covered houses, and streets bordered by crystalline trees and bushes made a lovely sight—sunsets and sunrises over icy mountains—indescribable. Driving in the "white stuff" though is another matter completely.

Funny thing, no matter how long people lived in the north country, the first snow always wreaked havoc, with cars running into each other, drivers getting stuck on hills, and generally behaving as if they had never seen snow before. After the first deep snow, the plows were out and the roads sanded.

In Alaska you had two choices: You could equip your vehicle with snow tires, don boots and gloves and a down filled parka, and get out there, or you could stay inside and gripe.

A good example of "getting out there" was the progressive dinner we attended three weeks before Christmas. The first hostess served the appetizers, then the party traveled to another home for the main dish. Imagine that, in minus-ten-degree weather with snow on the ground.

After dessert was served by the last hostess, we traded white elephant gifts. Frank had brought an exercise wheel—a sturdy wheel about four inches in diameter with a handle on each side. The idea was to kneel on the floor and hold on to the handles with both hands, put the body's entire weight on the wheel, then push yourself out to a prone position and back to the kneeling position.

"I hope none of our older members, like Ted McRoberts, winds up with this. He could get hurt," Frank had told me before we left home.

Sure enough, Ted, who was somewhere in his seventies, chose the bright package with the exercise wheel in it. Before anyone could stop him, he put his full weight on it, rolled to a prone position, and back up again. Frank and the younger men stared openmouthed.

We ceased to worry about Ted's physical condition. He had been a US Marshall in Bethel, Alaska in the 1930s and '40s, we learned later. As the months went on, we had an opportunity to get to know Ted better, but more about that later.

Christmas and New Years

A week or so before Christmas, one of our church members, Carl Herning—who had a homestead on Chena Hot Springs Road, about fifteen miles outside of Fairbanks—invited us to cut down a Christmas tree on his land. His wife, Mattie Lee, watched Ruthie, while Frank, Carl, and I tromped through the woods to find the perfect tree. It took a while, and we had a lot of fun. The tree chosen and tied to the top of the car, we joined the Hernings for hot chocolate.

The Christmas season and New Year's celebrations rushed by in a flurry of activities and gifts. Frank and I needn't have bothered to buy Ruthie anything—church members showered her with gifts. She couldn't have played with all the toys in a month of Sundays, but we accepted them graciously.

On New Year's Eve, the church had a watch night party, a party where church members celebrate with homespun fun. We ate, played board games and a few good-natured ones we made up, like the newlywed game though no couple there was a newlywed. As usual the hilarious outcome proved most married couples need to communicate better.

Nineteen seventy-seven came in as we prayed, sang a hymn, and closed with Auld Lang Syne. I wondered what the new year would bring.

*****

In January, one of our youth workers, a sergeant in the army, arranged for us to take the youth skiing at nearby slopes on Fort Wainwright. Most of the kids had been skiing at least once and were way ahead of us. Frank wisely decided to watch first; I did not.

The closest I'd been to a ski slope was *The Wide, Wide World of Sports* on TV. The back-and-forth technique to descend a slope had, unfortunately, not stuck in my mind I decided to try a run on the bunny slope and see what happened. How hard could it be?

My skis pointed straight down the hill, off I went. It was exhilarating, for the first ten seconds anyway, till, nearing the bottom, a landing was imminent. Somehow, no bones were broken when my body sprawled face first into the snow.

Luckily, for me, Mitch, one of the young men, saw my plight.

"Ms. Coder, Ms. Coder, that's not the way you do it," he shouted and skied over to help me up.

"I think I've figured that out, Mitch."

Frank joined me, and Mitch showed us how to swivel our skis from one side to the other, in a crisscross motion. It looked so easy when this young Adonis demonstrated it. We didn't master the slopes that day, took several more spills. However, we enjoyed the exhilaration of the skis gliding over the snow and the whoop-and-holler enthusiasm of our young friends.

One Sunday afternoon, Craig and Joy, friends from church, invited us to their cabin near Ester Dome. It was situated at the bottom of an extremely steep incline. Climbing down with our skis and baby Ruthie was challenging but doable.

We laughed and talked around a pot of chili. Then Craig and Frank watched Ruthie while Joy and I went snowshoeing. Snowshoes have a hardwood frame with rawhide lacings, and when walking on them, the weight is distributed over a large area to keep the feet from sinking. Snowshoeing is easy to learn, and I loved it. Later Frank, Craig, and I cross-country skied for a while. Exhilarating.

"I could ski for miles," I declared.

Since it was Sunday and we had the church music director and a youth worker with us, we had to leave for the evening service long before we wanted.

Craig and Joy had no trouble at all climbing back up the hill. I admired their stamina and did not want to admit my extreme fatigue. Frank carried the skis, but we forgot to move slowly and underestimated how hard it would be for me to climb carrying Ruthie. I almost passed out before I got to the top and collapsed onto the car seat. Only by sheer determination did I keep from losing my lunch. All my earlier outdoor-woman bravado vanished. Joy saw me and ran over.

"Clyta, I've never climbed that hill fast in deep snow carrying a baby. I'm so sorry. We should have helped you," she said .

No worries—I was young and quickly recovered.

Surrounded by Alaska's winter beauty—translucent icicles, clear days, and sparkling snow—we welcomed 1977 with new friends and work that we loved. I looked forward to learning more about pioneers like Ethyl Peasgood and Ted McRoberts.

Chapter 6

A Special Breed

> *Two are better than one...for if they fall, one will lift up the other.*
> —Ecclesiastes 4:9a, 10a

Come and meet some incredible men and women—a special breed of people who went to Alaska, faced the harsh realities of winter's darkness, cold and isolation, gloried in the midnight sun and chose to live there. They became our friends and blessed our lives.

Pioneer Woman

Ethyl Peasgood sat at the piano in the church sanctuary the day I first met her. A spry lady with grey curls and an infectious laugh, she had been the pianist at First Baptist Church since 1954. That was the year she moved to Fairbanks from "the bush"—what Alaskans call an isolated rural area. Ethyl taught the primary class in our Sunday school. She endeared herself to me one Saturday afternoon when she stopped by on her way home from the grocery store and found me in tears. Exhausted because the baby had kept me up all night, I had forgotten about the potluck dinner at church the next day and had nothing to fix. Ethyl looked in my cabinet. Unsatisfied, she opened the fridge and got out the milk, mayonnaise, an onion, and some carrots.

Smiling, she said, "I'll be right back." When she returned from the car, she had a jar of sweet pickles, a box of lime gelatin, and a carton of cottage cheese. "I'll give you my recipe for this gelatin salad and make something else. It's a great dish filled with so many good things."

That was Ethyl. She had a wonderful way of making others successful. I still have that recipe and refer to it as Ethyl's Gelatin Salad.

Now, more about this remarkable woman.

Ethyl had vowed she'd never go up in an airplane but that was before she decided to teach in the bush country of Alaska. In 1936, she flew with pilot Ralph Savory into Takotna, a village on the north bank of the Takotna River, approximately three hundred miles southwest of Fairbanks in the Kuskokwim mountains. There, she taught all the grades in a one-room log school. Her pupils included Athabascan Indians, Eskimos, and white children, all "eager learners who disliked having vacations."

Ethyl lived alone in an eight-by-twelve-foot room behind the schoolroom and cooked on a drum stove made out of a large steel barrel, holding her plate in her lap to eat. In winter, she chopped a hole in the ice to get water. On Sundays, she managed a combination church-Sunday school for ages one through eighty. Villagers often called on her to conduct funeral services.

This may sound like a hard life, but Ethyl said she loved it. She found the outdoor adventures exciting. In her own words, she said,

> Mushing a dog team, panning for gold, bear hunting, bagging spruce hen and ptarmigan with my .410 shotgun were all part of life in that little village. One summer I traveled the two-thousand-mile length of the Yukon River in all kinds of boats.

After four years in Takotna, Ethyl instructed the primary grades for twelve years in Bethel, a village further southwest, toward the Bering Sea. The only running water was pumped from the

Kuskokwim River, chlorinated, and delivered to homes by truck. One winter, because the water truck couldn't get through, the residents melted snow for several weeks, washing their hair, laundering clothes, and scrubbing the floor with the same water.

While in Bethel, Ethyl first lost the house she rented to fire then to flood, and later in Fairbanks she endured both experiences again.

For one year she taught all grades in Healy, in what had once been the Alaska Railroad depot. In 1953, she moved to Fairbanks to instruct first grade at Nordale Elementary for nineteen years. A former principal had once boasted that Ethyl, merely by her presence, could command the attention of squirmy six-year-olds when so hoarse she couldn't speak.

We met her after she retired, although even in retirement she served as church pianist, taught Sunday school, helped at the Native mission, and traveled the world. Ethyl never explained her teaching style to me. I learned from watching her that she loved children, accepted their individuality, taught them to respect her and to learn from and respect each other.

A peacemaker in the church, Ethyl often calmed the waters. I remember an incident when church members were ready to tar and feather a fellow congregant who had been indicted on moral grounds by local law enforcement. Ethyl suggested we pray for him, act in love and give things time to "come around right." Sure enough, the matter resolved itself when the couple's vocation took them to another town. In her wisdom, she counseled that Alaska residents came from all walks of life and we would not always agree on every issue.

Ethyl was a delight to know and a dear friend with whom I corresponded until her death a few years ago. She was one of the most contented women I have ever known though she had few material possessions and never owned a home. She rented a cozy one-bedroom apartment all the years she lived in Fairbanks until she moved to the Pioneer Home, a local retirement community. I will always be thankful to have known this wonderful lady.

A Man to Match Our Mountains

Ted McRoberts, Ethyl's best friend and a deacon in our church, was another of that special breed of "sourdoughs" we were blessed to know.

Ted was the man who had wowed everyone with his prowess on the exercise wheel that Frank brought to the Christmas party our first winter in Fairbanks. A retired US Marshall, he was no stranger to physical activity.

On two occasions in 1977, we had opportunity to hear more of Ted's story. One day after church, Ethyl invited Ted, Frank, and me over for sourdough pancakes and some of Ted's delicious homemade coconut syrup. Ted and Ethyl had met in Takotna, Alaska years before when he owned *The Kusko Times* and had interviewed her, the "local school marm." They never married but remained close friends. Ted told us how Ethyl, a self-reliant woman, had once grabbed his collar and pulled him out of the icy Kuskokwim, saving his life. Ethyl had told him, "Okay, Ted, that's one you owe me." [1]

"Ted, tell us a story about your life in the bush," Frank said.

"Well, I had decided that to be a real Alaskan, I had to kill a bear. No stranger to hunting, I took my .30–40 Krag rifle, walked up one of the dry glacial creeks, climbed a hill, and looking across the valley between two mountains, spied a black bear. I struggled up a steep forty-foot-high embankment, crawled over the top, and discovered I was less than ten feet from Mr. Bear who, from my prone position, looked ten feet tall. Without aiming, I quickly brought the rifle to my shoulder, fired, and watched the bear roll down the hill. I skinned the bear, cut a hunk of meat, and began the long pack back to town. I felt like "a real Alaskan."[2]

"What does bear meat taste like?" I asked.

"It's kind of greasy and stringy," Ted said. "That day it provided protein and nourishment that I wouldn't have had otherwise, so I was thankful to have it."

Frank invited Gene Medaris to read an excerpt from *North Country Marshal* at a Valentine's Day youth banquet. The book is an autobiography as told to Gene by Ted. Gene showed a picture of

Ted in full Marshall regalia. We listened to the heartfelt tale of Spud, the Marshal's First Deputy. Spud was part St. Bernard, part Springer Spaniel with an instinct for survival.

One rainy September night while on patrol, Ted realized Spud was no longer by his side. He called for him and heard the low growl, telling his owner something was wrong. When he reached Spud, Ted discovered an unconscious Eskimo man in a drainage ditch filled with icy water. Spud had dragged the man's body clear of the water and was straining to pull him out of the ditch.

In 1954, Ted went to Fairbanks to fill a vacant Marshal's post. He took his deputy, and they lived in a cabin where he and Spud could have the freedom of the woods. Spud went out one morning and didn't come back at breakfast time. Ted looked for him a long time. That afternoon, he saw Spud's tracks along the Chena River where ice had formed thirty feet out.

> I looked with horror as I realized the tracks led onto the ice but none led back.
>
> I was never a man given to tears, but the ache in my throat spoke grief words I could not say. All day my mind went back to the scene… maybe they weren't Spud's tracks! Maybe he would be in front of the cabin when I got home. I drove the distance home in hope. The front step was empty. I called Spud's name as I walked toward the door, but I knew they were empty words. Spud was gone.[3]

When Gene finished reading, Frank and I had tears in our eyes, along with everyone in the room, including Ted.

*****

Many years in Alaska had taught Ted how to live off the land. He told us the best places to pick rose hips and cranberries and how to use them. His recipe for cranberry/banana jam became well-known among my family and friends because on numerous occasions I have gifted them with this delicacy.

When Frank and I were going through a difficult time, our caring friend Ted came by one evening to encourage and pray with us. He told how his life had changed in 1937 when, through the witness of Ethyl Peasgood, he became a Christian. He shared how he knew that God watched over him and spared his life many times. I'll always remember his words: "Trust the Lord and he will always lead you in the way he wants you to go."

When Ted retired, US senator Ted Stevens paid him this tribute: he "was the Man to Match Our Mountains."[4] And, I might add, a real Alaskan.

Ted and Ethyl were a special breed who touched our lives and gifted us with friendship.

Recipes

Ethyl Peasgood's Gelatin Salad

1 large pkg. lime gelatin
2 tsp. carrots finely chopped
1 cup boiling water
2 T. sweet pickles
½ pound cottage cheese
½ Cup chopped celery
½ cup rich milk
2 T. onions chopped fine

Dissolve gelatin in boiling water and cool. Mix together remaining ingredients and add to gelatin when cool. Chill till firm.
*To make gelatin firmer, mix in 1 envelope Knox gelatin (a tip from my grandmother Clyta).

Ted McRoberts Cranberry/Banana Jam

Simmer for 10 minutes 3 cups mashed cranberries and 1 and ½ cups mashed bananas and 7 cups sugar. Bring mixture to a rolling boil and boil 1 minute. Turn off fire and add ½ bottle liquid pectin (Sure Jell or Certo) or 1 envelope Certo or 1 box powdered pectin. Stir and skim.

Pour into hot jars and lids and seal. Turn upside down for 5 minutes fruit won't all go to bottom. (Don't forget to set jars upright again or you'll have some "suspended jam"—I've done that.)

Yield- About 9 8 oz. jars.

CHAPTER 7

The Writing Life

Let the words of my mouth and the meditation of my heart be acceptable to you, O Lord, my rock and my redeemer.

—*Psalms 19:14*

Jimmy Bedford and I met at a December get-together of pastors and deacons. He headed the journalism department at the University of Alaska, Fairbanks. Professor Bedford, a wiry man of average build and sandy hair speckled with gray, smelled of fruity pipe tobacco and Old Spice.

"It's wonderful to meet you." I said.

"I've written some short stories and a sample youth Sunday school lesson. The Sunday School Board invited me to a writers' conference in Nashville." I sighed, and added, "When they learned my baby was due in July, it was decided that the writing schedule would be tough on a new mother and they suggested that I wait until next year. A big disappointment."

Professor Bedford paused to take a drink of his spiced tea. Setting the mug down, he said, "Why don't you enroll in Charles Keim's course, Magazine Article Writing. He'll encourage you to keep writing and to submit short articles, good practice for later assignments."

The acceptance of an article I wrote for *Home Life*, a religious publication, spurred me to enroll in the writing class at the University of Alaska. It met on Saturday mornings when Frank could stay with six-month-old Ruthie.

An excellent teacher and a journalist himself, Professor Keim taught us how to write a catchy lead sentence, how to study the markets, and how to write to an audience. He loved Alaska and knew that many in the lower forty-eight, as well as newcomers to the state and Fairbanks, wanted to learn more about living in the north country.

"You might write an article on Judge William Taylor. I believe he is a member of your church," he suggested in my scheduled consultation with him. The *Fairbanks Daily News-Miner* published my article "Cross-Country Dad" the week of Fathers' Day, 1977.

> President Jimmy Carter's recent memo to Cabinet members, urging them to spend more time with their families, found an advocate in Alaska Superior Court Judge Warren William Taylor of Fairbanks. Not only does he spend time with his family, he leads them in a year-round program of outdoor exercise—cross-country running and skiing.
>
> Judge Taylor's interest in running, in fact, developed when eldest son, Warren, took up cross-country skiing as a school event several years ago. Training for competition is easy in the winter. In summer though—tough skiing, no snow. The solution became evident, if you can't ski, you can run.
>
> To many newcomers, summer Alaska is too cool, windy, and rainy, and winter Alaska is unbearable. To the native Alaskan, the fresh summer wind is exuberant, and the icy winter air is a tonic. Families like the Taylors know they must become one with the arctic climate, the ice and snow. They must respect it, obey it, and, hence, be freed by it; or they will be paralyzed and imprisoned inside four walls six months of every

year, and, thus, defeated by it. The Taylors chose to be free—together.

Writing the story led to writing a column, "Coder's Comments," in T*he Alaska Baptist Messenger.* Alaska experiences were my theme with spiritual truths blended in.

For instance, one entitled "Bread of Life" described sourdough baking.

> A friend in Alaska offered to give me some starter for sourdough bread. I confess, I hadn't the slightest idea what she meant. Since then, I have eaten sourdough bread and pancakes—delicious. I'm not much of a baker, and I'll add another confession to the first: I've yet to do any sourdough baking. Maybe Erma Bombeck would say that's like admitting you don't own a Bundt pan.
>
> A dear friend of ours—an old "sourdough" himself—can trace his sourdough back to 1951. Of course, he doesn't have the original mixture. He's added to it and cultivated it as did the person who gave it to him, and before. Untouched, the starter would have died before it got started.
>
> A witness can likewise be passed on. In fact, unlike the starter, the good news of what Christ is doing in a life must be passed on again and again to remain fresh. If the bread of life is never offered to others, it will mold and die.
>
> Sourdough starter must also be cultivated in order to grow. Frequently it's necessary to add a little sugar or potato water to it. Or, if you bake bread often, you can pinch off a piece of dough each time, preserving it as starter. Spiritual life must also be fed and nourished in order to grow in the fullness of Christ. To have the bread of

life, a Christian must feed upon Him who is the bread of life.

Starter is kept in a covered crock. Hidden in such a container, the dough is protected and preserved. Hidden in Christ, the Christian is protected and preserved. Christ's protection offers a refuge from daily disappointments, big and little frustrations and temptations. (*Alaska Baptist Messenger*, October, 1978).

Another column entitled "A Bear behind Every Tree" referred to camping in Alaska. I compared my nonexistent bears with fears that never materialize and the importance of faith in God.

Every night I expected to see a bear claw coming through the canvass of our tent. Last May when we spent the night in a cabin, I couldn't sleep for all of the bears trying to get in the locked door. You're right, I have yet to meet "Mr. Bear." All of the bears were in my mind, nothing but imaginary enemies…

Most of my daily enemies are imaginary also. Starting with the ring of the alarm in the morning, time becomes an enemy because there is never enough of it. Each day I petition the Lord with a list of my enemies for him to conquer. I ask him to make everything all right between my neighbor and me, to convince my partner to do what I think he should, or to dig me out of an avalanche of responsibilities. These problems are very real. My fears about them, imaginary.

In John, chapter 12, Jesus rides into Jerusalem on a donkey as the crowd spreads palm leaves before Him and shout, "Hosanna" to claim Him as their King. In reading the passage, the hopes of the crowd came into focus. They wanted a King who could drive out their hated enemies, the Romans. They wanted a King to restore health and life and power to them. Like the well-meaning crowd, I often misunderstand the Savior's true nature. Though he came on a mission of peace, peace to the Jews meant conquered Romans. Jesus brought a peace born of love for all peoples, Romans as well as Jews.

The crowd wanted to be rid of all problems; Jesus wanted to go with them through their problems, changing problems into opportunities. They could not understand the Lord. Because they could not understand Him, they could not accept Him or His peace. (*The Alaska Baptist Messenger*, March, 1978).

I wrote articles for the *Alaska Baptist Messenger* until December 1978 and grew spiritually and as a writer in the process.

Insights

Writing the articles led me to deeper Bible study and meditation, planting seeds of peace in my heart that bore fruit in unexpected ways. An aha moment or clarifying moment, or whatever you want to call it, met me unexpectedly one afternoon. Rumblings from church members had reached Frank's ears. They mostly complained about the amount of time the pastor missed due to illness or because of his frequent trips to Tok to visit our mission pastor. Frank was also concerned, that often he and the pastor did not have time to sit down and plan together. He wanted to help Don by carrying more of the load.

A gnawing fear crept in to my heart—that once again something might go wrong and end our ministry. One day, I sat on the couch folding clothes. Frank and a deacon had gone to the basement of our house to look at a problem with the furnace. This particular deacon, one of the most negative people ever, often criticized church staff about nitpicky things like a time we forgot to turn off a light in the basement. Frank had voiced his irritation to me.

Give him patience, Lord, I prayed.

An ordinary day—no lights flashed, no angels appeared—I experienced no exaltation. In a down-to-earth voice, I heard, *"Disappointments will come, but I will be there with you."* I wondered, *Is there more, Lord?* No, that was it—a practical reminder to relax and let God handle the "how." In the months and years to come, I believe this practical statement prepared me to accept numerous reversals and to rest in God's presence.

CHAPTER 8

I'll Fly Away, Oh Glory

He said to them... Come away...and rest awhile...
—Mark 6:31

Anticipating a Trip "Outside"

Our days had been filled with work in the church, our daughter, Ruthie, and my writing. Now we needed to focus on our trip to the lower forty-eight. During those Alaska years, I learned firsthand how hard it is to live far from family when long-distance travel is so expensive. The church paid for Frank's expenses to attend a music workshop at Glorieta Baptist Conference grounds in New Mexico, and God provided generous friends who gave us a love offering to help with my airfare and other expenses. Our trip became a reality.

We had not seen our families in Arkansas and Oklahoma for three years, and we looked forward to our visit. I could already taste the fried chicken, watermelon, and homegrown tomatoes. Also, they would finally get to see Ruthie who would have her first birthday July 9.

Pan American's once-a-day flight departed Fairbanks at one o'clock in the morning, and Frank and I were already tired when we boarded. Ruthie, not happy about the change in her sleep cycle, cried most of the way, keeping us, and our unfortunate cabin mates, awake. A stern-looking woman across the aisle glared at me. I heard her comment to her seatmate, "Why can't the airlines put all the families with children in a separate part of the plane? I had planned to sleep tonight!"

The stewardess heard this and smiled at me. "Don't worry, most people understand and are sympathetic toward parents with crying infants. Could I warm a bottle for her?"

I handed her a bottle and said, "I fed her before we left, but warm milk might soothe her. Thanks."

That did the trick—at least for the next hour.

Frank's need to leave us in Denver and fly to Glorieta, New Mexico, for the music conference complicated our flight schedule. A long layover in Denver, then a short flight to Tulsa, Oklahoma loomed ahead for me. Angst over the long flight and part of it alone with a baby put a damper on my enthusiasm. To make matters worse, a well-meaning church member had told me of a friend whose Pan Am flight had been forced to land in the middle of the ocean. The woman had to slide down a makeshift ramp into a lifeboat. At the time I thought, *Oh great, just what I need to complete my flying paranoia!*

However, we landed safely in Seattle, changed planes, and boarded a Braniff jet bound for Denver. When offered champagne at nine thirty in the morning, we declined; we felt disoriented enough at that point. Ruthie finally went to sleep; but excitement, caffeine, and a donut sugar rush kept me awake.

In Denver, Frank had to hurry to make his connection and didn't have time to see me to the gate. He kissed me and gave me an anxious look.

"Now, why did I think that conference was such a good idea? I hate to leave you alone with the baby and all this stuff," he said.

"Go on," I said. "Once I get to the gate, I will be fine. The flight to Tulsa is only a couple of hours, then I'll be in the arms of family."

Ninety-plus temperatures combined with a Fourth of July weekend made the airport hot and crowded. An attendant explained that the air conditioning had malfunctioned and would soon be repaired. Not soon enough to suit me. I struggled with Ruthie in her carrier, a bulging diaper bag, and my purse. Seeing my dilemma, a porter hailed a transport vehicle to take me to the gate.

"Here you go, little lady."

"Thank you so much," I said and collapsed onto a seat.

Cool Alaska summers had spoiled me, causing me to forget about the Southwest's summer temperatures. They hovered at one hundred degrees our entire vacation.

Around seven o'clock that evening, Ruthie and I landed in Tulsa. For months I had imagined a waiting room full of family members with outstretched arms to welcome us home. Not one familiar face did I see. Tears stung my eyes, and weariness forced me to sit. They must have been delayed, I reasoned. Fifteen minutes went by then thirty. Ruthie woke up and began to fuss.

"Could I help you?" a flight attendant asked.

Between tears, I explained my plight. She offered to page my family. Maybe they had misunderstood the gate number. Fifteen more minutes passed, and no one responded. The attendant walked with me to a telephone and held Ruthie, while I called grandmother with whom we were to stay.

"Honey, your mother told me you'd be here tomorrow night. I'll call Millie and she'll get right over there," grandmother said.

The attendant took the phone and told grandmother the gate number, because by that time Ruthie howled in protest.

Later in grandmother's kitchen, after we hugged each other and shed a few happy tears, we unraveled the confusion. I had mistakenly written mother that I would arrive July 3, not July 2, and had not mentioned the day.

"I thought you meant Saturday, not Sunday," Mom said and smiled at me. I had a family reputation for getting my wires crossed.

Ruthie and I were exhausted when we got to bed around midnight and did not get to a sound sleep until early the next morning. We were snoring away when my sister Billie called and woke us about eight o'clock. Her voice welcomed me, but I would rather have been welcomed an hour later. However, this is the stuff family visits are made of. We all wished my eldest sister Carolyn and her family could have joined us, but they lived in Houston and were unable to be there.

*****

The week Frank spent in Glorieta, I attended a luncheon given by Fred and Juana Vandiver, longtime family friends and youth workers at Nogales Avenue Baptist Church where I had spent my teen years. I had lived away from Tulsa since 1966 and had not seen some of my friends since then, though I had known most of them since grade school. Over sandwiches, chips, sodas, and cookies, we caught up with each other's lives and exchanged pictures of our babies and news of mutual classmates.

Over and over I heard, "You mean, twenty degrees *below* zero—how can you stand it?"

"The cool summers are wonderful, never above seventy," I replied. Because it was July and near one hundred degrees outside. This riposte silenced all.

One night that week, I spoke to the Women's Missionary Union about church work in Alaska and shared the program with Joyce Cogburn, who told about her life in Guam. Two quite different ministries but both a part of Christ's body.

*****

Frank's dad; his stepmother, Elsie; sister Judy; and Grandmother Coder lived in Fort Smith, Arkansas. On our second week at home, Mr. Coder drove to Tulsa to take us to spend two weeks with the Coder family. He had told us, "I'll be there around ten." At eight o'clock Monday morning, I awakened to the jarring *brrrnng* of a persistent doorbell.

Ruthie somehow slept through the noise and Frank snored peacefully, so I grabbed my robe and stumbled to the door.

Not one for small talk, Dad Coder shouted, "Are ya ready? It's gettin' hotter by the minute so we need to get goin'."

With a hug and a big sigh, I urged him to come in while I woke Frank. He pulled on some pants, greeted his father, and they chatted over coffee while I changed Ruthie, fed and dressed her, and put her in the playpen. Frank and I ate a hasty bowl of cereal. Mr. Coder then whisked us out the door. Patience was definitely not his virtue.

The weather was just as hot in Fort Smith. That is, everywhere but in front of the air conditioning unit that blew a gale directly onto the kitchen table. Frank's Uncle Bud was visiting in the Coder household that summer, and he appeared at the table for each meal dressed in a leather motorcycle jacket.

"Robert," he would say, "if you're gonna keep it like the North Pole in here, this is what I'm wearing."

Mr. Coder refused to turn the fan off. Throw in Uncle Bud's tendency to take an opposite political stance, though he was a staunch Democrat like his brother, and mealtimes provided endless entertainment.

*****

We caught up with family and old friends at church while in Tulsa and Fort Smith. That made for a wonderful, but thoroughly exhausting, vacation. We would have been anxious to get back to Fairbanks and rest, except for one thing. During our stay in Fort Smith, we received a telephone call from Don Davis our pastor.

"I hated to call, Frank, but I think you might need to look around for a music minister's position. Some people think my health is keeping me from pastoral duties and that I need to resign. Without my support, you may not be able to remain on staff," he explained.

Frank turned pale, and I knew something not good had happened. "I'm sorry, Don, our prayer has been for your recovery. Let's pray that God will make a way for us both to stay."

After Frank told me what Don said, we sat in stunned silence, then I replied, "Probably it would be better not to tell the folks anything, because to be honest, we don't have all the facts."

Our friend Bill Canary, a native Arkansan, was visiting family in Springdale, Arkansas. He suggested we drive over to discuss the problem with him. Bill was director of the music and student ministries for the Alaska Baptist Convention.

We drove to Springdale and met Bill in a restaurant, happy to see his bright smile.

"Frank, this problem has brewed for a while," Bill said. "Most folks want Don to stay, but they know he can't handle the ministerial duties and that he could get better medical care in the lower forty-eight."

"I understand, but where does that leave me?"

Before Bill answered, he motioned for the waitress. "You know I would love to see you continue the music ministry in Alaska. The important thing is how *you* feel about returning."

The waitress refilled our cups. The pleasant aroma of coffee permeated the air, and the warm mug relieved the chill of the air-conditioned café. I glanced at Frank. He fingered the menu and slid his hand across the ceramic surface of the table then looked at Bill.

"More than anything I want to continue my ministry in Fairbanks and be successful."

"In that case, I urge you to return to Fairbanks as planned and try to work things out. Meanwhile, I'll be glad to help in any way and I promise to keep my ears open."

We prayed together. Our faith in God and friends like Bill equipped us to continue the Fairbanks ministry and to trust God to provide the way forward.

Time to bid our families goodbye came too soon. My grandmother, seventy-two at the time, had a pat answer she used every time we left Tulsa: "This will probably be the last time you'll see your pore ol' grandma." (She lived to be ninety-five.) My mother—who was more into our grand adventure—smiled, encouraged us, and shed a few tears. We reminded everyone that in October I would return with Ruthie on my way to Nashville and the Sunday school curriculum writers' conference. This brought a smile to their lips.

In private, Frank and I voiced our concerns. What would we face in Fairbanks? Would we be able to stay there?

Chapter 9

Hellos and Goodbyes

Do not neglect to show hospitality to strangers, for by doing that some have entertained angels without knowing it...

—Hebrews 13:2

Once on the plane from Tulsa to Dallas, I burst into tears. Frank held Ruthie to give me time to vent and compose.

The old tension tore at my heart: on the one hand, the comfort zone of family and friends in the lower forty-eight, and on the other, our ministry and friends in Alaska. Doubts and fears over our future in Fairbanks complicated the situation. All this poured forth in a torrent of tears. I closed my eyes to calm myself then took the now sleeping Ruthie.

"Thanks," I whispered and put my hand in Frank's.

"Better rest while she's sleeping," he said and added with a wry smile. "We have a few hours before we face the lions."

The remainder of our flight was uneventful. Pan American scheduled regular flights from Dallas to Fairbanks during the building of the trans-Alaska oil pipeline. On board with us were a mixture of military personnel, oil-pipeline workers, and tourists. Murmurs of subdued conversation alternated with the laughter and tears of infants and children.

*****

"Heavenly breeze," I said when we deplaned briefly in Anchorage.

"Feels wonderful," Frank agreed. He held Ruthie who squirmed, eager to try out her newfound talent, walking. Distant Chugach mountains, a smoky blue in the gloaming, welcomed us home.

Back in Fairbanks, we gloried in the cool Alaska temperatures, a relief after vacationing in the one-hundred-degree heat of Oklahoma and Arkansas. Par for the course—no downtime for us—a choir touring Alaska from California Baptist College would sing at the church the following Sunday. We graduated from CBC, and Frank had asked the choir to help celebrate publication of the new Baptist Hymnal. Helen Walker, the director, a petite woman and excellent musician, was our guest for the weekend.

Mrs. Walker and Frank talked on and on about the beauty of Alaska and church music in particular. Some of the new hymns in the hymnal graced the choir's concert on Sunday morning, but the choir, on a tight schedule, couldn't hang around for the evening service and caught a plane to Hawaii that afternoon.

Frank had chosen a long list of hymns for our choir and congregation to sing that night, many of them new to the organist. When the telephone rang, Frank answered, listened for a few minutes and frowned.

"No, not all, just do your best and I'm sorry I gave them to you so late. Since we returned from vacation Wednesday, I have struggled to catch up," he said.

He turned to me and added, "She's upset because she doesn't know ten of the hymns and hasn't had time to practice. I wanted to encourage the congregation to be more willing to sing new hymns instead of the usual top forty."

Because his voice rang with determination, I didn't mention that her irritation might be somewhat justified. "Maybe try to be more thoughtful in the future," I suggested.

The congregation enjoyed singing the new hymns, and Frank and I were relieved. However, we realized all problems were not resolved.

After the choir left, between the deacon body's discontent with the pastor and the organist's irritation with Frank, the climate at the church rivaled the Southwest heat we had recently endured.

Some members of the congregation felt the pastor's poor health prevented him from leading the church adequately, and we faced a long month of emotional discussion before Don resigned in September. Discouragement and sadness shadowed his close friends, but in dark times, God's blessings shine through if we look for them.

Beth was an accountant with the IRS and had secured a transfer to the Salinas, California office. A position with good pay awaited her. Don would have a chance to recover his health. Also the church wanted Frank to stay on as minister of music, youth, and education, with "added duties as required."

Even while under the stress of saying goodbye to a place they loved and dismantling a house, Don and Beth thought of us. One day, Beth knocked on my door.

"Clyta, I want you to have my portable Singer sewing machine. My mother gave it me, and it has served me well."

"Oh, Beth, this is so thoughtful, with all you have on your mind, you think of me. Thank you so much," I said. We hugged each other and cried a few tears.

"You know, this year didn't turn out like we had hoped, and we are concerned about you and Frank."

"Thank you, Beth, but I know God has a plan and will take care of us. Prayer is what we need…and we'll pray for you."

For every goodbye we said that summer there was another hello. Steven, Frank's younger brother, came for a visit in the midst of Don and Beth's leaving. A brown-haired eighteen-year-old, sixteen years younger than Frank, Steven was shy but he felt comfortable around us, and before long, Uncle Steve became a favorite of Ruthie's.

Frank huffed and puffed to keep up with him when they canoed the Chena River because Steve had worked as a camp counselor and outdoors guide in California and was in good shape. After he left us, Steven took the train from Fairbanks to Mount McKinley, a wonderful way to see Alaska. He camped and hiked in the park and fell in love with its wild beauty.

Steven had barely left when Ted and Irene Dunkle walked up our driveway. In the sixties, they had been stationed with us at Vandenberg Air Force Base, California. Frank was in his study, and for a few seconds, their names escaped me, but by the time they reached the door, my memory sharpened.

"Irene! Ted! How wonderful to see you! Do you live here now? How in the world did you find us?" I asked and ran to embrace them.

By the time they got inside, Frank had entered the living room.

"Well, I'll be darned," he said. His face was alight with happiness. "Ted, Irene."

He hugged each of them and welcomed them to our home.

"The air force assigned me to Ben Eilson for three years," Ted explained. "We heard through the grapevine that you had moved to Alaska, and the Convention Office directed us here."

A joyous reunion—we picked up where we left off in 1969 when they had tried to help us find a place to park our mobile home so we could attend California State University, Hayward.

"Remember that night in New Cuyama when our Volvo broke down and you drove from Vandenberg to rescue us?"

"That was a cold night!"

"We built a fire and roasted hot dogs before we left," added Irene.

In spite of our busy schedules, we saw them several times that year. Irene and Ted were part of our network of friends who moved a lot like us. We ran into them in unexpected places, and the world became smaller. Friends popping in relieved our homesickness.

*****

October rolled around, and I boarded the plane with Ruthie to fly to Tulsa for a week. During the week in Tulsa, Ruthie kept me up nights. Every morning when my seven-year-old nephew Jeff walked through the den, he found me asleep on the couch. One morning, he remarked to my sister Millie, "Boy, Aunt Clyta sure sleeps a lot."

After a week, I left Ruthie with Millie and flew to Nashville, Tennessee.

*****

At the writing conference, I received my assignment: write lessons for the pupils' book and lesson plans for the teacher. A minister was to write the exposition of the scripture passage and send it to me. He was a man of about forty, average height, neatly dressed.

My roommate introduced us. "Robert, this is Clyta Coder. She's assigned to your team to write the material for the pupil's book. She lives in Fairbanks, Alaska."

"Alaska! They flew you all the way from Alaska? Hmmm…uh. Excuse me, there's an editor I need to speak with." He turned away before I had time to reply, without shaking my hand or even a "nice to meet you."

"Whoa, guess he put me in my place," I said, half-jokingly.

"That's Robert Ballard. Don't let his rudeness bother you, and I might add, he's an excellent writer but a little slow getting the background material to you," Janet said.

Slow turned out to be a gross understatement. Not only did he *never* get his part to me on time, most lessons were not sent to me at all. About halfway through the project, I wanted to wring his ministerial neck. More about him later.

Other writers and editors at the conference were helpful and encouraging. Sharing ideas with fellow writers was invaluable. We were given a three-ring binder with information on lesson format, writing techniques, proofing our work, and other helps.

*****

Back in Tulsa, Ruthie was happy to see me again when I returned Thursday evening. Though Millie and her husband, Ron, had enjoyed caring for her, they were glad to see me because they had lost more than a few winks.

My flight to California to see Frank's Mom and family was scheduled the next day.

Goodbyes are never easy, but with only one day before my departure, we tried to be cheerful. The next afternoon everyone saw me off at the airport. It was a teary goodbye.

With only ten dollars in my pocket, I left Tulsa, The rest of my funds had been spent on a birthday present for Millie, in appreciation for her keeping Ruthie. Pride wouldn't let me borrow money, though any of my family would have been glad to help. The airline ticket was paid for and an in-flight meal provided, still it was foolish.

In Denver I was unable to reach my in-laws in California to tell them that the plane to Los Angeles had been delayed by two hours. I hoped they would read the flight schedule at the airport. Things would have gone smoother if the gate number had not changed also, resulting in a comedy of errors. An attendant paged my in-laws at one gate, but they were at another. After what seemed like hours, the attendant walked to another part of LA International and returned with Mom and Tom. Our explanations were muffled amid hugs and howls from Ruthie who, at this point, had plainly "had it."

For the most part, we had a pleasant stay except that Ruthie caught a virus, probably from crawling around on the airport floor. Children bounce back quickly however, and we did not have to delay our departure. This time, I swallowed my pride and borrowed money from Mom Dennin to cover any needs on the last leg of our journey.

Once more, I said goodbyes to loved ones and anticipated Alaska hellos.

Babies and Stencils Don't Mix

City lights lent a luminescence to the snowflakes that filled the air as the plane landed in Fairbanks. Ruthie had slept during the flight from Seattle, and I had grabbed a quick nap.

"So glad you're home. I sure missed my girls." Frank embraced us in a bear hug, as I stepped into the airport. He kissed Ruthie on the forehead before putting her down to let her run off steam after her airplane confinement.

Over dinner, he brought me up to date on local happenings. Since the pastor's resignation, the buck stopped with Frank. He had to assume the administration of the church.

"Half of the deacons are happy with my work—the music selection, visitation, and the varied youth activities. They're hopeful about the future of the church, but the other half complains about every little thing," he said.

"Frustrating, I know," I said and put my hand on his arm. "Let's give it more time. You are adjusting to carrying the load without a pastor, and the congregation is adjusting to you." We sat awhile in compatible silence.

"Have any women called about the Women's Missionary Union conference this Saturday?" I asked.

He rolled his eyes. "Several."

Because I was the Associational Women's Missionary Union director, I had seen to many conference details before I left for Tulsa, but now I needed to tie up any loose ends. This kept me hopping for the rest of the week. To add to the confusion, Saturday morning Frank needed help with the church bulletin.

A. B. Dick mimeograph machines ranked right after mumps and measles on my favorites list. Only because my husband was desperate did I agree to tackle the bulletin.

Ruthie had to stay with me because Frank had a meeting that morning. The playpen placed close to the desk allowed me to type and watch her at the same time. The first page of the bulletin finished and placed on the desk, I lifted Ruthie out to change her diaper and didn't notice the stencil fall into the play pen when I set her back down. About halfway through the second page, I glanced at Ruthie to discover she had found the dropped stencil, crumpled it, and now her hands, face, and clothes were ink-stained blue.

"Oh, no!" I yelled, lifting her and trying in vain to hold her away from me. She succeeded in placing a few inky handprints in places I won't mention. Also, the indelible ink stained my hands as well. Fortunately, about that time, Sherry, a young friend who lived across the street from the church, stopped by for a chat.

"Look at you two," she said. "Could you use some help?"

"Definitely," I replied, explaining that I was caught between the church bulletin and a meeting to host within the hour.

Sherry could be a pill sometimes, but she was an excellent typist. She took over, and I drove home to clean up and prepare for the conference. Except for a ruined blouse, an ink-stained baby, and blue hands, all was well and the sessions went off without a hitch. No one asked about my hands. Most of the pastors' wives had wrestled with church bulletins themselves. After that, Sherry volunteered to type and duplicate anything the church needed. Yeah!

In November, Van and Wanda Bowman invited everyone to their home for Thanksgiving. Through the picture window, we watched dusk settle over the green spruce trees and the new fallen snow, though it was only three o'clock in the afternoon. The short daylight hours reminded me of the brevity and fragility of friendships. We gathered to eat and give thanks for the blessings we shared and to pray for our friends, Don and Beth Davis, their new life in California, and for our own families scattered across the lower forty-eight.

After dinner, the dominoes came out, and Van played the guitar and sang his favorite song, "The Tennessee Stud." Those less enterprising took a nap. Ruthie slept on my lap, while Frank relaxed in a chair in front of the cheerful fireplace. Caring friends sat scattered around the room. We had much to be thankful for.

CHAPTER 10

Uncertain Days

The steadfast love of the Lord never ceases, his mercies never come to an end; they are new every morning, great is your faithfulness.
—*Lamentations 3:22–23*

Frigid weather in December contributed special lighting effects to the Christmas program.

Due to twenty-below temperatures, Fairbanks's electrical circuits became overloaded and caused frequent blackouts. Frank was singing the bass aria from Handel's *Messiah* entitled "The People That Walked in Darkness," when the lights went out. Complete silence enveloped the congregation. We sat suspended in time and absorbed the message of the prophet Isaiah's words, while Frank sang bravely to the end. Because no electricity meant no heat either, he quickly closed the service with the congregation and choir singing the first verse of "Silent Night."

We spent Christmas that year with close friends Fred and Melba Pelosi and their daughter, Kim, all members of our church. Melba taught business courses at the University of Alaska. Her husband, Fred, an army officer during the Second World War, received disability retirement. His strong bass voice and his beautiful prayers blessed the congregation. They encouraged us many times that winter and always welcomed us into their home.

Winter Blues

I now had to get down to business writing the youth Sunday school lessons assigned to me. Lesson one was due in Nashville the first day of February. To write and to care for a two-year-old wasn't easy, and deadlines proved to be a challenge. Now that she could walk, Ruthe didn't want to stay in her playpen. If I spent a few minutes each morning with her, she played, and I could write for maybe an hour, and for another hour during her afternoon nap.

Adult colleagues are harder to control. My bigger challenge was getting the minister who wrote the exposition of the scripture passages to send them to me on time.

A call in February to the editor of youth Sunday school curriculum in Nashville got a response. "I'll speak with Reverend Ballard and ask him to send the material two weeks before the deadline," he said. However, the next deadline came and went with no lessons received.

"That egotistical preacher," I complained.

"Study the commentaries and write based on your understanding of the passages," Frank suggested.

Sound advice, if I had not been so stubborn. Instead, I chose to outline each lesson, make notes, and wait for Reverend Ballard's background material to write the lessons. A couple of times, he sent the material a few weeks before the due date, and I only missed the deadlines by a few days. Most of the time, he sent nothing at all. Frustration and resentment prevented me from seeking God's direction at this point, which is *always* what He wants us to do.

There was no time to dwell on this, however, because other things needed my attention. Frank developed an infection that resisted the antibiotics prescribed. The combination of ill health, winter's harsh temperatures, and brief daylight hours made for some dark days.

A bright spot was that the pastor search committee had some promising applicants. One minister had been invited to speak at an associational meeting and was to be interviewed by the committee. He turned out to be a flashy man who dressed like a car salesman in a loud red-and-blue plaid blazer and who preached a sermon full of his own accomplishments with little spiritual substance. His wife sang and referred often to her friendship with Wanda Jackson, a well-known country and Western recording artist. The couple hoped to find a church in Alaska that would allow them to have a television ministry like they had in Oklahoma.

"Flash might impress the congregation, but he doesn't impress me," Frank said when we returned home from the associational meeting.

"Me, either. I wonder why he wants to leave Oklahoma."

"Exactly. He hardly looked at the church yesterday, asked no questions about the congregation's goals, and was vague about his own vision of ministry."

A lot of questions remained unanswered. If we tried to discuss them with the personnel committee, deacons, or other church members, we received harsh criticism.

Frank came home one day in March looking pale and drawn. Since Ruthie was still napping, I handed him a cup of coffee and sat down.

"Okay, let's have it, I said."

"The chairman of the deacons says I haven't kept regular office hours, nor made efforts to bring more people into the church and hinted that when they call a new pastor, the congregation might not be able to afford two salaries. Also—same song, second verse—some members don't like the music chosen and want to hear more of the old hymns and less of the 'dirges.'"

What they referred to were his choice of hymns such as "In the Cross of Christ I Glory" or "Be Thou My Vision," rather than more familiar selections like "The Old Rugged Cross" and songs written by gospel composers.

We sat in silence for a few minutes, then he added, "And the church wants to extend a call to the preacher who spoke at the associational meeting a few weeks ago."

"Well, you know without a permanent minister, church attendance declines and church finances, too. A new pastor might help," I suggested.

"Maybe, but not him" he said. "What we need is stability, not a television evangelist."

Frank left to go back to the office, and I sat to ponder all that we had discussed and prayed for the Lord's guidance.

One evening a few weeks later, Frank turned to me with misty eyes and said, "Maybe I'm not cut out to be a church music minister. A teaching certificate might be the answer."

In April, he resigned after several unpleasant encounters and a monthly business meeting, airing the aforementioned complaints.

A New Twist

After his resignation, close friends dropped by to pray with us and lend support. A friend loaned us his truck and camper for a mini-vacation to relax and renew our spirits. We decided Frank would drive the camper to meet me after the women's retreat the last weekend in April.

The associational women's retreat was to be held at a campground near Birch Lake, about fifty miles from Fairbanks. Birch Lake is a beautiful area with tall pines, mountains in the distance, and spring wildflowers pushing up through the not-quite-thawed ground. Approximately fifty women came together, sleeping bags in tow, to relax and visit with friends. The women didn't get to see each other often due to distance, harsh weather, and busy schedules. Each group of women brought a part of the food—their own munchies—and helped with meal preparation and cleanup. We heard two inspiring talks by Ruth Meeks, a longtime Alaska resident and owner of a bookstore in Anchorage, then the women talked and laughed until the wee hours.

The next morning, my queasy stomach and scratchy throat made me question whether going camping after the retreat was a good idea. A moot point since this was before the age of cell phones, and Frank was on his way to meet me.

As it turned out, the weather warmed up a tad, to about fifty degrees, and we enjoyed hiking and exploring the area around the lake. Frank toted Ruthie in a carrier on his back. She loved that.

I was okay as long as we stopped now and then and rested. That night, our toddler bounced around in her bed till about midnight then joined us in our already crowded bunk and prevented us from sleeping. During the night, I felt more nauseated and did not feel much better the next day.

*****

Back in Fairbanks on Monday, the doctor confirmed my suspicion: in addition to a pure-dee-old cold, I was pregnant.

Not the best timing. Frank had enrolled at the University of Alaska to complete a teaching certificate. He had some GI bill funds left to draw from, but not enough to live on. We hated the thought of leaving Ruthie with a sitter, but my return to the workforce appeared imminent. What we needed was a big helping of faith in God's provision.

My responsibilities as Associational WMU director helped me focus on God's plan rather than my present confusion. Until the Baptist State Convention in August, I remained in office and therefore was a member of the State Missions Committee. Our committee was responsible for writing materials for the State Missions Offering that included the Season of Prayer coming up in September 1978. The committee met and decided to ask the missionaries to write a letter telling us how gifts from the 1977 offering had blessed their work. We asked them to share their dreams and prayer requests and to describe their ministries. The replies we received reveal the dedication of these men and women and illustrate aspects of life in Alaska.

From Selawik, an Eskimo village near the Bering Strait, Harley and Martha Shields wrote,

> We want to thank the folks for helping us buy a wood stove for the church...it will save on fuel costs... Martha and I are responsible for the five missions of Kotzebue First Baptist Church: Selawik, Kiana, Ambler, Shungnak, and Kobuk. We minister to Selawik and Kiana on Sunday to

the other three on weekdays. We travel by airplane (Cessna 180), snow machine, and boat. We pray for Eskimo men and women and young folks [who have] a vision for their own people.

Donald Rollins shared this information on his ministry on the Alaskan Peninsula near Katmai National Park:

This year our plans call for development of new mission work between King Salmon and Cold Bay. We need a church building in Ekwok before Fall and we plan to expand our work in Koliganek... The Lord is working mightily in our area. We are planning vacation Bible schools for four other villages. Pray that we reach many of the more permanent local people.

Valeria Sherard wrote the following prayer requests for Friendship Native Mission:

For wisdom and strength and guidance in the best way to use my time. For dedicated and committed volunteer workers. For the Christian Eskimos—that their Christian growth will lead them to become workers and strong in their faith and conviction. For workers with the native students at the University. For Eskimo families in Fairbanks who are lost and hopeless, with family, drug, and alcohol problems.

Reading the letters inspired me and encouraged me to pray for others and trust God for the needs of my family.

*****

Our first need was a place to live.

One day, Carl Herning, a member of First Baptist, invited us to his home at five-mile Chena Hot Springs Road, about fifteen miles north of Fairbanks. Carl and his brother had come north in 1938 and homesteaded. He cleared land and built a lovely log cabin home on the edge of a large meadow surrounded by white birch trees. In the past, he had managed the transportation system for the school district, doing mechanical maintenance on the busses and housing them in a large bus barn on his property.

"You'll have to move out of the house supplied by the church," Carl said. "Mattie Lee and I have a mobile home that's empty since my son moved. Come on, I'll show you." We walked up a flagstone path over fern-covered ground interspersed with trees. The mobile home was spacious, well-insulated, and had a combination kitchen/dining area, a living room, two bedrooms, and two bathrooms.

"Carl, this is a beautiful place," I said.

"We'd love to live here," Frank added. How much do you need to charge?"

Carl only wanted us to pay utilities, not rent, because that would foul up his income tax. We couldn't believe our luck, except we knew it wasn't luck, but God's provision through friends who cared.

I wondered what the rest of the year would bring.

Chapter 11

That's What Friends Are For

Then Samuel took a stone and set it up…and named it Ebenezer, for he said, "Thus far the Lord has helped us."

—*1 Samuel 7:12*

Frank was introspective and withdrawn for a few months after he resigned as minister of music at the church.

"You know, your life has touched a lot of people young and old," I reminded him. Pastor Don's resignation last summer and the confusion that followed made your job harder."

"My mind knows. My heart is not ready to accept. Give me time," Frank said.

Reality bit. He was unemployed, and because he desired to earn a teaching credential, and could only work part-time. I needed to get a job. My pregnancy made this more complicated. In addition, for me to be a working mother had never been part of our child-rearing plans.

J. D. Back, the pastor at Friendship Mission, was a friend of ours. He and his wife, Jenny, worked alongside missionary Valeria Sherard. They ministered to Native Americans of Eskimo, Aleut, and Athabascan Indian descent. He prayed with us and understood when Frank said he wasn't ready to attend church again or be around people. I attended services each Sunday and often on Wednesday night, uplifted by the friendship and acceptance of the loving congregation.

Frank soon decided that staying home to sulk wasn't helpful to him or me either and attended with me.

Worship in this new setting without the pressures of a staff position allowed us time to regain our balance. Letters from home also helped us to have the serenity to accept the things we could not change, as Reinhold Niebuhr states in his beautiful prayer. Mother read between the lines of my letter that told about Frank's resignation from the church and his decision to get a teaching certificate.

"It was hard for me to leave five young children to go to work," she wrote in answer. "Each day I left you in God's hands, put one foot in front of the other, and trusted Him to lead the way."

So, I got up, put one foot in front of the other, and trusted God to lead the way. Wanda Bowman and Melba Pelosi, friends from First Baptist, offered to watch Ruthie while I went for interviews. A medical clinic advertised for a clerk to type workman's compensation forms and letters, and I interviewed and got the job. Ruthie was with Frank much of the time, and when he was in class, Wanda and Melba kept her. Although their kindness lifted a weight from my shoulders, not being with my little girl grieved me.

*****

When you go through difficulties, you learn who your real friends are. We met Owen and Linda Fansler when they joined First Baptist a month before Frank resigned. They were tall Texans, friendly, and easy to talk to. He was a pilot in the air force, and she was a nurse. They helped us move and invited us into their home for meals.

The Fanslers had a daughter—Darcie, about Ruthie's age—and were expecting a baby in July. Together we planned a picnic at a campground near the Chena River one evening in early June. The air was cool, not cold, and islands of blue sky with a hint of sunshine peered between gray clouds. We adults relaxed around the fire after stuffing ourselves with wieners and marshmallows, while the girls romped and laughed nearby.

"I catch you," Darcie shouted to Ruthie. Giggles followed, then Darcie screamed as she slipped and fell into the river.

"Darcie," Owen and Linda shouted. Their faces paled, and Owen plunged into the water, followed by Frank. Moments later, the three of them emerged, teeth chattering.

Hypothermia was a danger. Water temperature even in June hovered slightly above freezing, no floating ice, but still frigid.

"Thank God you're safe," Linda said, holding Darcie to her.

Darcie shivered, as Linda pulled off her wet clothes. We carried extra clothes and blankets in our cars, a customary precaution in Alaska. Owen and Frank changed into dry clothes, and Linda wrapped Darcie in a blanket and held her. We got in our cars and turned on the heaters.

Later that night, Linda telephone to tell us, "Darcie was asleep by the time we reached home, no harm done."

"She's fine," I told Frank after hanging up the phone.

He took a deep breath and let it out. "That's the important thing."

*****

In any situation, acceptance is key. Once we adjusted to our new routine, things were easier. We had plenty of time to enjoy the outdoors since the sun shone until eleven or twelve o'clock at night. Carl Hernings's homestead where we lived was a fairyland of lacy fern amid slender white birch trees. In the meadow grew wild roses, snow-white Canadian dogwood and magenta clusters of fireweed. A more peaceful place to live could not exist. The only drawback was the fifteen-mile distance from my job in Fairbanks, the University of Alaska, and church. However, we saw this merely as an added challenge.

*****

Life moved on and carried us with it. Still, uncertainty clouded our future that summer. We waited for a baby to come, waited for

Frank to complete coursework for a teacher's certificate, waited to find out where he would teach. Because I knew the clerk-typist position was a stopgap measure until the baby came, it was hard for me to face work each day. Soon my obvious pregnancy would force me to tell Jan Wiese, my boss, that I was pregnant. Not to worry, though. She had seen a stream of clerk-typists come and go, and because she took it in stride, I relaxed.

Frank did his practice teaching at West Valley High School that fall with band director, George Wiese. So now my boss's husband was my husband's boss. We all laughed over the coincidence. George and Jan had both come to Alaska in the mid-sixties, fell in love with it, and made it their home.

*****

Soon it was the end of August. Summer had vanished; autumn brought her palette to paint the leaves orange, gold, and red. The color lasted only a brief time, and if you winked, you missed it.

"Let's go for a drive out the Steese Highway toward Chatanika to see the fall color," Frank said one Sunday afternoon. He didn't have to ask me twice.

We grabbed our jackets and headed out. White birch trees graced the road; their orange and golden leaves danced in the sunlight.

"Why don't we stop and have a bite to eat?" Frank said when we saw the sign for the Chatanika Roadhouse.

He pulled in near a creek with a wooden bridge. We walked up a path that lead to the rustic roadhouse and laughed and talked as we strolled, savoring the brisk air. Golden leaves carpeted the ground, and a lighthearted glow filled my heart. Inside the roadhouse, the fireplace crackled and filled the air with a woodsy aroma—perfect to sit near with a piece of warm apple pie and hot cider.

Sometimes my heart retreats to live that day again.

Autumn leaves were not the only changes in our lives. Ruthie had to spend most of the day with a sitter because Frank attended class and taught long hours. We did not want to impose on the friends who kept her for short times during the summer. The situation was difficult but temporary.

A more positive change brightened my schedule. My friend Valeria Sherard led a program of children's activities at Friendship Mission. She coordinated a ministry to children of Eskimo, Aleut, and Athabascan descent. It was hard to get teachers, and I wanted to volunteer, but Frank had a class on Monday evenings and couldn't stay with Ruthie.

However, we worked out a plan whereby I collected Ruthie and fixed a simple meal in the mission kitchen, then Frank went to his evening class. Ruthie played with other toddlers, and I taught Bible stories, songs, and crafts to lively eight- to ten-year-old girls who blessed me and took my mind off the uncertain future.

Valeria was a single woman who had smoky blue eyes and dark hair streaked with gray. Her soft voice and strong accent immediately told anyone listening that she was from the deep South, Mississippi as it turned out. We became close friends. Her compassion and patience influenced my relationships with people and my teaching style.

In mid-October, we adjusted to more change when Moose Creek Baptist Church asked Frank to direct a Christmas cantata. Moose Creek was a settlement a few miles from Ben Eilson Air Force Base and twenty miles southeast of Fairbanks. Frank agreed to help, with the understanding that his time was limited. Neither the church nor he realized how limited.

Every Sunday for the next month, we drove ten miles from our home on Chena Hot Springs Road to Moose Creek. After the morning service, we ate lunch with Pastor Ed Conners, his wife, Virginia (not their real names), two of his sons, and three young airmen. I was eight months pregnant and needed to rest in the afternoon, while Frank had choir practice. The last thing two-year-old Ruthie wanted was a nap. Sometimes I was successful in convincing her otherwise.

Frank balanced his music ministry with practice teaching and an evening class. Because he faced graduation in January with no job in sight, he began to research possible teaching opportunities. He applied for a position, teaching music to students kinder through high school in Cordova, Alaska. The Cordova School Board was interested, but they needed him to be on the job the Monday after Thanksgiving.

Cordova is not on an island, and though it is only about one hundred miles from Anchorage, no road goes there; it's fly from Fairbanks or take the ferry from Valdez.

An uneasy feeling about such a move at this time troubled me.

"Frank, you have to complete the coursework for your credential and you made a commitment to work with the church choir," I reminded him one evening.

Three or four open music books and a daily plan book lay scattered across the kitchen table where Frank worked on lesson plans. In between, he doodled on scratch paper, then crumpled his artistry into spheres and dropped them on the floor. Ruthie clapped her hands and laughed as she retrieved them and threw them toward the wastebasket.

"The academic dean will give me permission to finish the coursework early and the pianist at Moose Creek can practice with the church choir until my return for Christmas break," he replied.

I tried again. "Besides, your phone interview didn't give you much information. There are so many unknowns about the Cordova position. For instance, I wonder why the teacher resigned in October and why they can't use a substitute until January so they could interview you in person. Wouldn't it be better for us if you substituted here this spring and applied for a position next fall?"

"They need me now and I think I can make it work," he replied in a tight voice. The muscles in his neck tensed.

"Well, how nice. I guess it doesn't matter that the baby is due any minute and I have two-year-old Ruthie to care for." My voice rose in anger. "Not to mention that I have to drive over snow and ice for fifteen miles to work every day. How can you be so insensitive?"

Frank threw up his hands. "You forget that I need a job in January to provide for this family," he shouted.

I sank into a chair, covered my face with my hands, and cried—a woman's last defense. My shoulders shook with long pent up frustration. Frank let me vent until I calmed down. He pulled me to him and said, "Leaving you right now is hard, but I've got to have a job and don't know what else to do. I'll be back in a few weeks for Christmas break. Then, you, Ruthie, and the baby will go to Cordova with me."

After several long conversations and much prayer, it was easier to view the situation from his perspective. He had a family to support and was anxious to begin teaching. This made him impatient and unable to see the broad picture. Once more, the Serenity Prayer came to the rescue, and I accepted the things that could not be changed.

*****

The Sunday morning after Thanksgiving, amid a lot of hugging, kissing, and tears, I trusted him to Wien Air Alaska, the plane with the man in the fur parka painted on the side.

Afterward, I drove to church rather than go home to be depressed. Ed and Virginia insisted I stay for lunch before driving home.

The next few weeks were tough. Ruthie missed her daddy, and exhaustion was my companion much of the time. Still, with acceptance of the situation came a peace and a strength not my own. An old gospel song speaks of *leaning on the everlasting arms*—and so I leaned.

*****

Carl, our landlord, put up the Maverick at night in the old bus barn, started it for me each morning, and made sure it was in good running condition. I don't know what I would have done without the help that he and Mattie Lee gave me that month. An incident with Ruthie revealed how fragile my emotions were.

One morning, Ruthie cried, "Mommy boot, Mommy boot," when she climbed into the car seat. She was bundled in snowsuit and mittens, and since it was almost time for me to be at work, I ignored her. Poor child. One of her boots had fallen off before she got in the car. She still had her shoes, but only one boot, and I failed to notice this until we reached the sitters. Not much I could do about it then.

That evening, Carl handed me the boot and said, "I bet that was a cold little foot."

Tears began to flow, and I couldn't stop them. "She could have gotten frostbite. What kind of a mother am I?"

Carl put his hand on my shoulder. "You're a fine mother. Come on in the house and have dinner with us and a cup of hot tea and everything will look better."

He was right. Seated in their living room in front of the fireplace, feet elevated on a hassock, I drank a cup of tea and thanked God for sending friends willing to share my load.

Surprise! I'm Coming!

In the next few weeks, helping hands supported me.

"Clyta, how's it going?" Linda asked one evening when she telephoned.

"I feel good, really, just tired."

"Get some rest and don't worry. If the baby comes before December 28, I'll be happy to stay with you at the hospital." Linda assured me.

"Thanks, Linda. Don't know what I'd do without all my friends." I looked forward to Frank's return and my last day at work.

A colleague whose apartment was on my way to work offered to ride with me each day and help get Ruthie up the stairs to the sitters.

"Thanks, I'll feel safer having someone in the car with me," I said, smiling.

"It's you who should be thanked. I've been walking to the clinic," she responded. The gratitude in her voice was thanks enough for I knew she was a single mother having a hard time. She turned to look out the window. I saw a tear slide down her cheek.

*****

On Sunday, December 17, the temperature dropped and the church service at Moose Creek lasted longer than usual. The car wouldn't start when I got ready to leave.

"The motor needs to be plugged in for a few hours, Clyta," Ed said.

"Why don't you and Ruthie stay for lunch and afterward I'll watch her while you rest. After the evening service, I'll drive you home and Ed can follow in your car," Virginia said.

"You two are such a help. Thanks so much."

That night, the air was frigid, but at least the roads were clear. I prayed they would stay that way for my last week of work and Frank's homecoming.

Winter changed her mind on Monday. The temperature warmed, and it snowed all day and into the night. The children's Christmas program at the mission that evening was a success. Joseph and Mary in their homemade costumes looked fondly at baby Jesus while cotton-ball-adorned sheep and shepherds in bathrobes looked on. A cherub choir of cute four-and-five-year-olds ended it with a cheerful song.

"We wish you a Merry Christmas. We wish you a Merry Christmas and a Happy New Year"

After the program, Valeria said, "Clyta, I don't feel good about y'all driving fifteen miles back home, too dangerous. My couch turns into a bed. Why don't you and Ruthie stay in town with me?"

My weary body agreed, and I accepted her invitation.

The overheated apartment made sleeping difficult. Ruthie missed her bed, and neither of us slept much. Somehow, I made it through the next day.

Tuesday night was no better. Even a two-year-old recognizes when change is in the air. Ruthie slept fitfully. When she woke up for the third time, I put her in bed with me. Still, a squirmy toddler and a rather large girth kept me from getting into a comfortable position.

The next day was Wednesday, December 20. The women in the office had decorated the break room in pink and blue streamers for a brief baby shower that morning. I had told them diapers were the greatest need, and they responded generously.

"Thanks so much. The new little one will be well-diapered," I said.

The baby was not due until December 28, but by noon, it looked as though he or she might make an early entrance.

An uncomfortable backache was my biggest complaint. I rested during lunch, and later Jan, my boss, urged me to go upstairs to see the obstetrician, who examined me and told me to call my husband and get to the hospital.

"Doctor, Frank is teaching in Cordova, and he may not be able to get here in time. My friend, Linda, is prepared to stay with me. The hospital isn't far. I can drive myself there."

The doctor stared at me wide-eyed. "No, you will *not* drive yourself. My nurse will take you to the hospital. Now, go call your husband and make arrangements with your friend."

Ruthie's birth had been long and hard. The prospect of another exhausting ordeal increased my anxiety, especially knowing my husband might not be with me. Even so, the calm assurance that my life and my baby were in God's hands gave me strength and readiness to face whatever came.

*****

The school secretary in Cordova got Frank to the phone in a hurry when she heard the situation.

"What? The baby's not due yet, and there's no plane today," Frank sputtered when told the news. He had neglected to tell me that air service in and out of Cordova was available only on alternate days.

Exasperated, I said, "The baby doesn't know it's supposed to wait until the twenty-eighth, and we're both sorry we didn't choose a day when there's a plane you can catch. The nurse will drive me to the hospital. Linda's going to meet me there after she takes Ruthie to her house."

"Oh, God, I feel awful," Frank said. "You know I wanted to be there."

"Yes, and I didn't mean to snap at you."

"She'll be fine, Mr. Coder," I heard the school secretary assure him. "Don't worry."

"She's right, Frank. I feel good except for a backache. Linda can call you with progress reports and give you the hospital phone number. Talk to you later."

"Well…okay. I love you."

"Love you too."

After I hung up the phone, Jan and the other typists offered to carry baby gifts to my car. It dawned on me that the Maverick couldn't stay parked at the clinic all night. One lady volunteered to drive it to her house, but when told that not only was it a standard transmission vehicle, but the shifting pattern was backwards, she stared at me in disbelief and withdrew her offer. Jan's husband drove it to their house for Frank to collect later.

Doctors in Alaska encouraged expectant mothers who didn't live close to the hospital to keep a packed bag in the car with everything they would need after delivery. Following this advice proved to be a good idea.

The nurse supported my arm as we walked to her car, our heavy boots crunching the snow underfoot. Huge snowflakes caught in our fur-lined parkas and filled the sky. She drove me through the winter wonderland to bring a new life into the world.

*****

A nurse took me right to a room when I arrived at the hospital. Linda, and I were prepared for a tough night, but so far, there had been only twinges of discomfort, no pain except for the backache, and that was not severe. Linda arrived and told me Ruthie was playing happily when she left her with Owen and Darcie and Kevin.

"Oh, good. You and Owen have been such a help."

Linda coached me on breathing techniques while I rested. The contractions were closer together, but were not painful, merely a little uncomfortable.

The doctor came in to check me. When finished, she said, "Almost fully dilated, let's go to delivery."

"You're kidding. The contractions weren't that strong."

Everything moved rapidly. I lost track of time, but sometime later the doctor told me to give a hard push, and Jeanne Marie Coder made her entrance into the world, a painless delivery except for a backache and a few cramps. Honest!

"The Lord knew Frank couldn't be here, so he gave me a special blessing tonight," I said. The emotion of the day left me drained yet filled me with a warm glow.

Linda smiled and patted my hand. "I'm glad you had an easy time."

"You and the baby were simply ready," the doctor said.

The Lord and I knew better.

They wheeled me to a room about nine o'clock. My roommate, a Catholic, teased me. "With a name like Jeanne Marie, she will surely be a saint."

The nurse chuckled at this, then suggested I rest.

Before I could call Frank to tell him the good news, he called me.

"How's it going?" he asked in a shaky voice.

Feeling rather smug about the whole thing I replied, "You remember we agreed on the name Jeanne Marie for a girl? Well, Jeanne Marie joined us about thirty minutes ago—you have a new daughter."

"Already? You're kidding. That's wonderful…already? Are you all right?"

"Yes. Exhausted, but happy."

"I love you…I need to call the folks… But, wow…already? And me not there." He rambled on—clearly in worse shape than I.

"Kiss her for me and I'll see you tomorrow," he added.

Tomorrow. I breathed easier. We would be together again—Frank and I, our new baby, and sister Ruthie.

*****

Frank arrived Thursday afternoon on the four o'clock plane, collected Ruthie from Owen and Linda, and came to the hospital.

"Mama," Ruthie cried. Dressed in her bright red snowsuit, she ran to me and laid her head on my arm.

My husband kissed me and held me tight. The fur on his parka tickled my nose.

"You look wonderful," he said, taking the baby from me. "Well, hello there little one." He kissed her gently on the cheek and let her grasp his finger with her tiny fist. "She's a beauty—all red and wrinkled," he added, grinning.

I drew Ruthie close. "Here's your new sister."

"Baby," Ruthie said. She gently touched Jeanne's cheek and looked at her with wonder in her eyes.

*****

By Christmas Eve, we were new-baby tired, except, of course for Ruthie who had boundless energy or baby Jeanne who chose to be awake anytime we needed to sleep. Christmas morning was clear, about minus twenty degrees with three to four inches of snow on the ground. In Alaska, we never had to rely on dreams for a white Christmas.

About nine o'clock on Christmas morning, I called Linda Fansler.

"Linda, the baby kept us up most of the night. Maybe we shouldn't try to get together for Christmas dinner."

"Please, no," Linda pleaded. "Owen and I were up with Kevin too! Oh, Christmas alone would be too depressing. The turkey and dressing and veggies are about done, and you said Mattie Lee gave you a pie. We can take turns eating and dozing off."

And that's what we did. We weren't a lively crowd, but we found comfort in being together.

Ready to head North to Alaska

CLYTA CODER

Peace River Valley, British Columbia, Canada

Russian Orthodox Church, Kenai, Alaska

Kenai Messiah Chorus, 1976

MOUNTAINS, RAINBOWS AND AN OCCASIONAL MOOSE

ALTOS JOIN IN--Cecilia Meyer, Ami Rediske, Karen Syvrud.

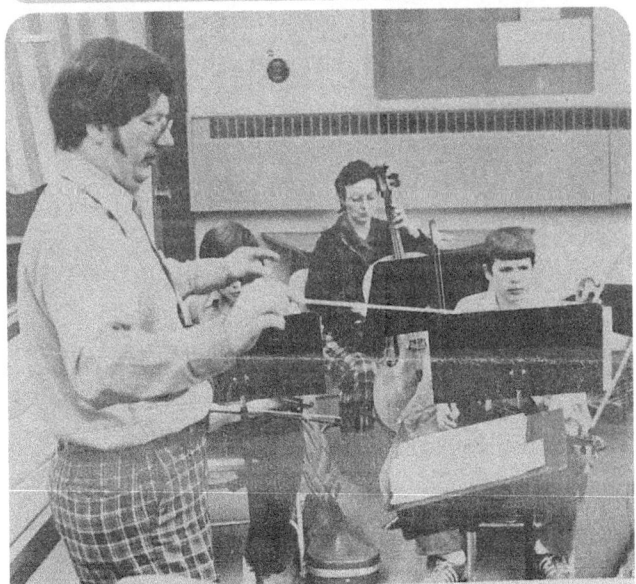

STRING SUPPORT—Frank Coder leads as Toby Jones (behind Coder), Karen Hornaday and Peter Rosheger accompany on strings.

Kenai Messiah Chorus, 1976

First Baptist Church, Kenai

Ethyl Peasgood is shown here beside a Woodley Airlines plane at the Takotna airstrip in the spring of 1938.

Ethyl Peasgood and her pupils pose on the steps of their Bethel schoolhouse.

When Alaska celebrated its centennial as a part of the United States after being purchased from Russia in 1867, it was fitting that a North Country Marshal be a part of it all. Here Ted and Ethyl wave from the back of a rail passenger car used by President Harding on his visit to Territorial Alaska. The car is now a permanent part of the Alaskaland exhibition in Fairbanks.

Ted McRoberts and Ethyl Peasgood (1967, North Country Marshall, page 143)

A golden autumn day my heart returns to, near Fairbanks

Our closest Alaska friends—Owen and Linda Fansler

MOUNTAINS, RAINBOWS AND AN OCCASIONAL MOOSE

Ferry from Valdez to Cordova

(Cordova) Frank reading to Ruth nd Jeanne

Cordova friends-Pastor Richard Harding and wife, Susan, Nancy and John

Ruthie not impressed by the moose, near Cordova

Bear Walking by Steven Dennin's campsite at Katmai National Park

CLYTA CODER

Glennallen – Clyta, Ruthie and Jeanne

MOUNTAINS, RAINBOWS AND AN OCCASIONAL MOOSE

Uncle Steve Dennin, Ruthie and Jeanne "on the road again" to the lower 48 in our Frank-built camper

Travel on the edge—near Fort Nelson, British, Columbia.
"We wanted to go, our Volvo didn't"

CHAPTER 12

Fairbanks Farewell

The eternal God is thy refuge, and underneath are the everlasting arms…
—*Deuteronomy 33:27a (KJV)*

Frank had to be back on the job in Cordova January 3, giving us only six days to pack before we left to catch the ferry in Valdez. Our landlord suggested we box things we couldn't take and leave them in one of the bedrooms. That would save us the trouble of packing everything since no one would live in the mobile home that year.

"Clyta, we want to give you a baby shower before you leave," the Women's Missionary Union president told me the day after Christmas.

One-hundred to-dos popped into my mind, and I wanted to shout no. Instead, I said, "How thoughtful of everyone, Margie. I appreciate your offer so much. Our limited space and time is the problem. I've already been given two showers. We have more clothes than the baby could possibly wear and only until December 31 to pack."

"Believe me, honey, I have tried to explain all that to the women, but it's like herding cats. They want to have a combination shower and fellowship after prayer meeting Wednesday night. From my experience as an air force wife, probably the best idea would be to smile, thank them, and pack only what you need. Later you could pass the clothes on."

Wise advice. She gave me a wink and a hug and headed out the door.

About thirty women, and a few men, gathered Wednesday evening with gifts of diapers, onesies, bibs, cute little dresses, and toiletry items. More practical friends gave money. Graciously I thanked them all. Because we lacked space to take all of the clothes to Cordova, Jeanne never got to wear most of them—frustrating—although the money was a godsend, and the diapers came in handy.

*****

Frank had rented the empty Episcopal parsonage in Cordova. The house was furnished with a stove, refrigerator, washer and dryer, dining room furniture, and a bed for Ruthie. On Friday, Owen Fansler helped Frank load the homemade trailer with his desk, our clothes, bed, household items, and the baby's crib. We hoped our semi-reliable 1968 Volvo would prove sufficient to the task.

While they worked, I cajoled Ruthie into taking a nap. I ate a sandwich and lay on the couch to rest. Sometime later, a hand gently nudged my shoulder, and I looked up to see Linda Fansler smiling down at me.

"Clyta, I brought over dinner—meatloaf, potatoes, salad, and cookies—I knew you'd be exhausted by now. It's only been nine days since you had a baby."

"Girl, you always know the right thing to do. Thanks. Can ya'll join us?"

"No, a neighbor is watching the kids, so I'll have to get back. The food is in disposable containers, and I would have sent it with Owen, but it wasn't ready. We probably won't be able to come back over tomorrow, so I guess this is goodbye for a while."

I stood up and hugged her. She hadn't removed her parka, and the wolf trim on the hood brushed my cheek. Tears clouded our eyes. "Yes, bye for now, Linda, and thanks."

*****

MOUNTAINS, RAINBOWS AND AN OCCASIONAL MOOSE

On Sunday, December 31, Mattie Lee entertained Ruthie with a tea party, and Jeanne slept while we finished packing. About four o'clock that afternoon, we loaded the babies into the car and prepared to leave. The weather had warmed to around ten degrees above zero. Snow had just begun to fall and threatened to become heavier. Carl tried to talk Frank into waiting until morning. However, Frank wanted to hit the road. Carl, one of the most generous men I have ever met, reached into his pocket, his eyes moist.

"Frank, take this. You might need it," he said, handing him a fifty-dollar bill.

"Carl, I don't know how to thank you."

"No thanks needed. Be careful and take care of that little family of yours." He hugged us all, and we took off.

Carl always kept the winding gravel road to the highway plowed and in good condition. A clear road for the ninety-eight miles to Delta was a blessing—the heavy load made travel hazardous enough. The no-frills motel room in Delta was clean, though small, and it was the only accommodation in town. After a quick breakfast of cereal and sweet rolls the next morning, Frank went to check on the car.

"Guess what…the car won't start," he said when he returned.

"You're kidding, won't even turn over?"

"Nope. I don't know what to do. No garage will be open on New Year's Day." We sat in silence for a few minutes. "Ray Nelson is the pastor at the Delta church. Maybe he can help."

"He will if he can," I said with confidence.

Frank tried to call Ray, repeatedly getting a busy signal. The name of a local Delta resident with whom I had served on an associational committee came to mind, and I found him listed in the old telephone book.

"Let me call Jim. He's a member at the Delta church. Maybe Ray's phone isn't working." Overwhelmed by fatigue, a new baby and a move, my voice broke when I tried to speak. Frank took the phone.

"Jim, sorry to bother you, this is Frank Coder. I used to be the youth director at First Baptist…yes, in Fairbanks. We're on the way to Valdez to catch the ferry tomorrow and having car trouble. I've tried to phone Ray Nelson, but can't get through"

Frank replaced the receiver. "Jim said he'll come to take us to Ray's house. He placed a hand on my shoulder. "Thanks for your help. I know this is hard on you, but everything will be okay. Ray's a good mechanic."

I managed a weak smile.

Jim took us to the parsonage. On the way he explained, "The person who shares Ray's party line tied up the phone for an hour or so. Jane said it happens all the time."

Later, he, Ray, and Frank towed the car to the house, and the motel owner agreed to let us leave the trailer until the car was repaired.

Ray and Jane—seasoned Alaskans who followed the north country rule of open hands, open hearts—fed us a delicious breakfast of bacon, eggs, sourdough pancakes, and moose sausage. Jane and I caught up on each other's lives, and she entertained Ruthie and watched the baby while I rested. A bed at the Ritz Carlton couldn't have felt better.

The heated garage enabled the men to work more efficiently. Heated garages are a huge blessing because automotive parts are no fun to handle in subarctic Alaskan temperatures when gloveless fingers are numb with cold. The temperature outside had dropped to minus twenty degrees under clear skies. The men repaired the problem in a few hours, something to do with moisture, though I never understood what exactly.

Frank shook hands with Ray and Jim and thanked them. "I don't know what we would have done without you."

"Breakfast was delicious and that hour of rest made me a new person," I told Jane.

"Glad to help," Jane said. She and Ray clasped ours hands, and we formed a circle.

Ray prayed for our safe travel and asked the Lord to guide us in our new life in Cordova.

The Volvo was equipped with good snow tires that provided traction on the icy roads to Valdez. The next morning, a blue sky with bright sunshine turned the snow into sparkling jewels. Our spirits lifted as we drove toward the ferry dock.

Though the past several months had been stressful, God's everlasting arms had supported me and my family.

Chapter 13

Moving On

> *For the Lord will go before you, and the God of Israel will be your rear guard.*
> —Isaiah 52:12b

Our day started early on the morning of January 2 when we boarded the Alaska State Ferry Aurora for its biweekly voyage to Cordova. Icy mountain peaks bid us farewell from the Valdez harbor. Small islands of ice floated by, translucent in the bright sunlight. The water's surface flashed like blue-green sapphires. Alaska wore her winter beauty.

We drove onto the ferry, parked our car below, and walked up to the passenger deck to sit in comfortable chairs. A queue already formed at the concession stand where travelers could purchase snacks.

"Mattie Lee packed us some sandwiches. Closer to lunchtime we can get drinks," I said to Frank.

"Good idea." He stretched out on a bench to rest.

Ruthie had awakened at five o'clock that morning, so I made her a pallet, and the motion of the ferry lulled her to sleep. Eleven-day-old Jeanne slept in her carrier. The anticipation of seeing a new place, meeting new people, and the caffeine from two cups of coffee kept me awake and overcame new-baby fatigue.

Fellow passengers included three or four family groups, some Native American. They sat in chairs around the large glass enclosed deck. The deck was well-heated as if to defy the arctic chill outside. We dressed comfortably in jeans, sweaters, and sweatshirts; heavy parkas, jackets, and boots strewn on chairs added to the relaxed atmosphere. The hum of family conversation joined the drone of the engine.

"We should reach *Tatitlek* in about an hour," a woman told her young son, who repeatedly asked the familiar question, "Are we there yet?" This told me we would make a stop at the Alutiq (ah-loo'-tik) village about thirty miles south of Valdez on the eastern side of the Tatitlek Narrows.

The population of Tatitlek ranged between 80 and 120 people who depended on commercial fishing for halibut and salmon. The location of the village had been moved several times. Between 1898 and 1913, the townsite was located at nearby Ellamar where the copper mine employed one hundred men. But when the mine closed, loss of employment led the people to resettle on the present town site.

Sure enough, about an hour from Valdez, the ferry approached the village, and two families disembarked. From the ferry, we saw several frame houses and a small white Russian Orthodox Church nestled approximately fifty yards from the water at the foot of a snow-rippled mountain.

I turned to Frank who had awakened by this time. "What would life be like in such an isolated place?"

"Pretty quiet I imagine, but Cordova isn't exactly a metropolis either."

"Right. We'll probably miss being able to drive to Anchorage or Fairbanks anytime we wish. since no road connects Cordova to a highway.

So far, we had lived in the Southcentral Alaskan town of Kenai, with a population of about five thousand, most employed by the oil industry, and Fairbanks, an interior town of six thousand with two military bases, Alaska University and a fairly diverse population. Temperatures in Fairbanks could dip to minus sixty degrees in winter—minus twenty was not unheard of in Kenai. We had been told that Cordova didn't veer much below zero.

Jeanne and Ruthie who wanted to be fed, interrupted our musings. Frank bought some juice and sodas and got Ruthie settled with a peanut butter and jelly sandwich. He sat beside her to eat his own sandwich. I found a private place to nurse Jeanne, and she happily went back to sleep.

As we neared our destination, I thought about the mixed blessing of this move to Cordova. Frank would have a fresh start in his new vocation as a music teacher for the Copper River School District. We had emerged fairly sane from the last hectic months in Fairbanks and were blessed with two healthy children. A comfortable house awaited us in Cordova, a pretty coastal town with a mild climate. Family and friends were praying for us in Alaska and in the lower forty-eight.

Frank could leave the stresses of the ministry behind him. However, church work was a known, Cordova and teaching an unknown. That's what worried me. *Were we jumping out of the frying pan into the fire?* Excited but almost afraid to be excited described our state of mind.

We arrived at the Cordova Ferry Terminal. "Wow! Such colorful boats moored at the harbor—red, blue, green," I said, as we drove down the ramp toward our new home.

"Blue boats," Ruthie parroted. "Pretty boats."

We left the harbor and headed to the grocery store, passing an ice cream parlor, a ladies' boutique, the hospital, and the post office. A comparison might be the opening scene of the TV series *Northern Exposure*, with or without the moose walking by.

"Welcome back, Mr. Coder," the owner of K&E Foodland greeted us. A friendly, smiley woman, she was short with grey-streaked brown hair.

"Mrs. Ekemo, this is my wife, Clyta, our two-year old, Ruthie, and baby Jeanne."

Ruthie hid behind her dad, while Jeanne slept blissfully as only newborns can.

"Beautiful children. Please call me May," she said with a smile and shook my hand. "Pastor Harding plans to stop by with groceries but let me help you with some staples."

"I'm glad to meet you, May, and thanks, that would be great. Frank's told me how friendly everyone is." Soon the cart held bread, milk, butter, eggs, bacon, cereal, and other basic needs.

"We can deliver groceries for a while—till you get on your feet; in fact, they will be delivered today…y'all look exhausted." Mrs. Ekemo, I learned later, sometimes lapsed into the Southern accent she brought from Georgia.

*****

We drove up Lake Street to the vacated Episcopal parsonage, only minutes from the town center. The diocese had been happy to rent it to us until they moved a new priest to Cordova. Frank deposited Ruthie and me at the front door leading into the second story. He kept the baby with him and drove around to park the car in the back of the house at basement level.

We had been in the house only a few minutes when Richard Harding, the Baptist pastor, arrived with a chicken casserole, veggies, and a chocolate cake plus a box of groceries. A six-footer like Frank, he smiled a lot and had a friendly demeanor. Frank and Richard put together the crib and our bed. The twin bed in Ruthie's room came with the house and was already assembled. Since Frank needed to report to work the next day, we fed the children and ourselves and went to bed.

Settling In

We had brought in our luggage with enough clothes for a few days, toiletries, necessities for the baby, toys for Ruthie, plus a couple of cooking pans. That helped, although no one can foresee how much stuff a family needs each day. My approach— take care of the children, and get a few items at a time from the trailer. Climbing up and down the stairs several times a day, not to mention trying to keep Ruthie from tumbling down them, became a constant challenge. Wouldn't you know, we lived in two-story houses when each baby was born.

Our new house had a small but well-equipped kitchen, two baths, and three bedrooms. On Saturday morning, Frank donned work boots.

"I'll unload the rest of the furniture and household goods. Sorry I couldn't get to it sooner."

"Thanks. I'll miss running back and forth to the trailer—such good exercise," I teased.

Community Baptist Church

Early Sunday morning snow began to fall. It floated down like feathers falling from the sky, as we entered the church building.

"Good morning, Frank, and you must be Clyta," Susan, the pastor's wife, greeted us. She led me to a table filled with cookies and coffee and helped me get settled. "Did Frank tell you we're having a potluck after church? Hope you all can stay."

"That will be nice, though I didn't bring anything," I said.

"Good heavens, don't worry about that. We're just glad you have the energy to attend church so soon after the baby, and a move too." She patted my hand.

We realized from the start that the members of Community Baptist Church in Cordova were a caring congregation. Richard Harding and Robert Varnum ministered as co-pastors. Richard's wife, Susan, directed the Community Christian Center, an ecumenical outreach to the people of Cordova. Betty, Robert's wife, directed the preschool. They also shared the parsonage as one family, along with the Harding children, Nancy and John. Church members referred to them as the Harding-Varnums.

Not only did they see to it that we had a hot meal the evening we arrived and groceries to boot, but Susan offered to pick me up for Tuesday morning Bible study and keep the girls for a Mother's Day Out every Friday. We didn't know at the time what an encouragement they would be to us.

Community Baptist was affiliated with the American Baptist Convention. The ABC had been organized as the Northern Baptist Convention during the Civil War. Frank and I had always attended and served Southern Baptist Churches If we had any misgivings about this at all, they were soon dispelled by the overwhelming warm spirit alive in the congregation.

History of Cordova

Sam, one of the young teachers, befriended us. He was a history buff who knew a lot about Cordova, and he joined us for dinner on several occasions.

"Tell us about the town, Sam. Why the name, Cordova?" I said.

"Don Salvador Fidalgo, a Spanish explorer, named the site Puerto Cordova in 1790. The Eyak tribe were the sole inhabitants of the area until European fishermen came and developed a fish camp and cannery site," Sam explained.

"What about the Kennecot mines?"

"When mining began, the townsite was chosen as the railroad terminus and ocean shipping port for the copper ore. A guy named Michael J. Heney, builder of the Copper River and Northwestern Railway, named the town, and it was moved from Eyak Lake to the shore of Orca inlet in 1908. He also built the Copper River and Northwestern Railway."

"Was it a successful mine?" I asked.

"Very. Between 1911 and 1938, when the mine closed, more than two hundred million tons of copper ore was transported through Cordova."

Sam was knowledgeable about many things and we became good friends.

*****

Perhaps if we had been younger when we lived in Cordova, not having a TV and only limited radio station programming might have been harder, but I loved to read, and Cordova had a decent public library. KLAM broadcasted country-Western, pop music, and news from eight o'clock in the morning to two o'clock in the afternoon. The evening session featured a series of old radio programs like *The Shadow* and *Jack Benny* from six o'clock to ten o'clock in the evening. Frank depended on his stereo and record collection for the classical music he enjoyed. At that time, because there was no theatre in

Cordova, frequently a movie was shown in the high school auditorium or at the library.

*****

A few weeks after we arrived in Cordova, the pastors invited us to their home for a late dinner following the Friday night basketball game. The high school band was to play a few selections at the game. Frank planned to come for the children and me afterward. He arrived much earlier than expected and strode past me without a word.

"Okay, let's have it. What's the problem?" I asked.

"Only a handful of kids came to the game, and they played a ragged version of *Peter Gunn*. Two boys didn't show, though I warned them this morning that it would affect their grades if they didn't come. We were supposed to perform another number, but I decided against it."

"You did encourage the ones who came, I hope."

"Oh yeah, I thanked the faithful few, gave them a pep talk, and told them to enjoy the game."

"Give things a chance to work. They need to get used to you. Anyway, dinner at the pastors' home will be a welcome treat."

"I'm tired and don't really feel like going anywhere tonight."

"Oh, please, honey, let's go. I've looked forward to it all day. They're fun to be with. And Susan's a teacher who knows the kids and might have some advice," I argued. When he saw how much it meant to me, he agreed to go.

Susan, an awesome cook, had prepared one of the most mouthwatering clam casseroles I have ever tasted—with Alaskan King Crabs of course. Unfortunately, I've lost my recipe and have never found another that tastes as good. After supper, the women chatted together in one end of the den, while the pastors and Frank discussed the mechanical problems Richard was having with his car.

Nancy, the pastor's daughter, joined us when we gathered for coffee and dessert. Frank and I admired her spunk. She had severe scoliosis and had to wear a steel brace from neck to lower back. She wore it with a smile, and I never heard her complain.

"Nancy, thanks for playing tonight," Frank said.

"Sure, Mr. Coder. I'm glad you didn't make us wear those funny uniforms. Yukk, that ugly green. We would have looked like frogs," Nancy replied.

Frank laughed. After Nancy had excused herself and gone to her room, Frank turned to Susan. "Guess you heard things didn't go well," he said, looking glum.

"Don't get discouraged. It's never easy to start in the middle of the year."

"Right," agreed Richard. "And you inherited a difficult situation."

He referred to the fact that the students really liked the teacher who had resigned in November due to a feud between administrators.

"I want this job to work out. We'd like to stay here," answered Frank.

"Maybe because of that, you feel the pressure and are trying too hard. Try to relax and enjoy the kids," offered Susan.

Although Frank didn't reply, I hoped with all hope that he would take her advice.

Iceworm Festival

A fun diversion from school the next weekend was the annual Cordova Ice Worm Festival. Always held the first weekend in February, the celebration originated in 1961 to offer locals a break from the long bleak winter, although the day of the festival dawned bright and clear. The celebration was named for a species of worm found only in Alaska, British Columbia, and parts of Washington and Oregon.[2]

"Look, Daddy. Snake! Snake!" shouted Ruthie, her blue eyes big with wonder. "It has lots of legs."

"It sure does. Come on, let's find a good place to stand."

Frank and Ruthie joined the crowd to watch the fifty-foot ice worm meander down Main Street. Fifty or more children and teenagers walked underneath the long tunnel-like float made of blue fabric stretched over large circular wire segments. The dragon head made the ice worm look like a long Chinese New Year's dragon. The crowd cheered as the ice worm zigzagged along stopping now and then to bow. When it bowed too close to Ruthie, it frightened her and she began to cry, so Frank brought her inside to me at the popcorn machine sponsored by the community center.

During the wee hours of the morning, the church staff had made donuts to offer free to parade-watchers. In 1979, the festival had craft and food booths, a local bluegrass band, skits, and door prizes.

The next weekend, Valentine's Day, gave an opportunity for more fun and fellowship. The pastor rented *Good-bye, Mr. Chips* for a family night movie. The camaraderie of the Iceworm Festival and the fellowship of church members helped Frank and me to relax into life in Cordova and feel more positive about our future there.

CHAPTER 14

Stormy Weather

And the peace of God, which surpasses all understanding, will guard your hearts and your minds in Christ Jesus.
—Philippians 4:7

The first two weeks in February, the students, with the support of the school faculty, responded better to Frank and his teaching methods. A couple of them stopped by his classroom to help him organize music and told him they were enjoying band. However, when grades came out, problems began to multiply.

Frank gave Ds to the two ringleaders of the band students who failed to show up to play at the basketball game. Even students who had always made As got lower grades because Frank believed in giving As only for exceptionally high achievement. This proved to be a very unpopular move. The students also felt that the former teacher was dismissed unfairly, and they resented his being replaced.

A few teens demonstrated their displeasure by trashing the band hall and destroying a set of drums. The next week, expensive audio-visual equipment was broken. A week later, the attacks became more personal.

One evening after supper, the sound of shattered glass startled us. We ran to the living room and found a large rock with jagged edges lying on the floor below the window. Glass shards surrounded the rock. Thirty minutes earlier, Ruthie had played in that same spot.

Frank slammed his palm hard against the door facing. "Those little creeps. It's one thing to tear up the school, but when they come at my family...I'll—"

"You think you know who did it?"

"Only a strong suspicion. Anyway, I'm calling the police. This can't go on."

"Why are people treating us this way?" My voice shook with emotion.

Ten minutes later, a young police officer arrived. "Sergeant Martin[1]," he said, extending his hand.

Frank showed him the window. "We were in the dining room working on lesson plans and reading when we heard the glass and ran in here to find this. I think it's probably the same boys who destroyed the drums and the audio-visual equipment at school, but none of the kids will admit to seeing them."

"Do the boys have something against you?"

"Yes. Their grades, which could have been raised if they'd played at the basketball game. Their attendance is spotty and punctuated by mouthing off. I gave them Ds, though they deserved to fail."

"Those boys have caused trouble before," Sergeant Martin said after Frank gave him the names. "Most of the youth here are hard working kids who work alongside their parents. Sometimes they don't see the value of an education if they feel it doesn't relate to seining for salmon. Let me know if you think of anything else or see anything suspicious. Cordova is usually a peaceful town, and I'd like to keep it that way."

A couple of weeks later, the car drove a little rough on the way to Bible study. I ignored it because the tires were old.

Later, Frank walked home for lunch and stormed into the house. "You didn't drive the car with the tires like that did you?" he demanded.

"Like what?"

---

[1] The sergeant's name has been changed.

He glared at me and shouted, "Both rear tires have been slashed. You didn't notice? I'll have to walk back to school now. I'll call Sergeant Martin and tell him." He gulped his lunch and left.

The children napped on, so I slipped out to see the damaged car. Sure enough, both tires were flat and bore jagged knife wounds. *How did that escape me?*

Stress. Moving eleven days after having a baby, the broken window, the hostility shown by the students—all of it caused me to be nervous and distracted. Taking the children to Tulsa for a visit seemed an option, but to leave my husband to deal with the problems alone didn't feel right.

Frank struggled to be positive. Often, he couldn't sleep, and a few days earlier while reading a story to Ruthie, he had stopped mid-sentence to stare blankly. The trauma of moving from job to job weighed on him; this was the fourth one in six years, and it wasn't working out either. He felt a failure, and I believed he experienced situational depression, even thoughts of suicide. I didn't know how to help him, and often fear and frustration robbed me of peace and caused anxiety and resentment.

After walking outside to look at the tires, I reentered the house, got down on my knees, and poured my heart out to the Lord, seeking wisdom for Frank and for myself. Taking my Bible, I searched the book of Philippians. So many verses in that beautiful book speak of the apostle Paul's joy in Christ, in spite of the harsh circumstances in his life. Theologians believe he wrote it in Rome, after he was released from prison and lived in a house chained to a soldier. How could he be joyful in such a dismal situation? Yet as I read through his epistle, the encouraging words calmed me.

> Yes, and I will continue to rejoice for I know that through your prayers and the help of the spirit of Jesus Christ, this will turn out for my deliverance. (Philippians 1:19)
>
> Rejoice in the Lord always, again I will say, Rejoice… Do not worry about anything, but in everything by prayer and supplication with

thanksgiving, let your requests be made known to God. And the peace of God, which surpasses all understanding, will guard your hearts and your minds in Christ Jesus. (Philippians 4:4, 6–7)

The familiar words spoke to me. In the face of assault by angry students, we could claim the "peace that passes all understanding," just as Paul had when beaten and chained to a prison guard. I asked God to help us forgive the persons who harbored such hostility and to give me wisdom in our relationship.

The situation worsened before it improved. In April, a band from West Valley High School in Fairbanks was to come to Cordova to give a concert. A few days before they arrived, someone shattered the windshield of our car. Again, no one saw who did it. Frank faced the humiliation of having to explain the broken windshield to George Wiese, the band director and his practice-teaching mentor.

"Looks like you probably won't want to stay here next year," George said. "Sorry you're having such a rough time. I'll do my best to help you get another position."

*****

The next night at the Cordova High School gymnasium, the high-pitched voices of excited teenagers and the honking of trumpets and trombones met my ears. Smells of floor polish and popcorn, mixed with perfume and perspiration, greeted me. Ruthie and I were dressed in warm pants and jackets, Jeanne bundled in a onesie and a thick blanket. April in Southeast Alaska was still chilly.

Trumpet bells gleamed like brass in the bright lights, students looked spiffy in crisp white shirts and blouses and black pants and skirts. The gym grew warm from the heat of multiple bodies.

Ruthie sat with a responsible high school girl, while I climbed up a few rows and placed Jeanne next to me to remove my jacket. The baby carrier was made of slick plastic with a loose buckle on the strap. We were three or four feet up—and the benches were narrow—not a good idea to set her there.

As I tugged at my sleeve, I saw Jeanne fall through the large space between the bleachers to the floor below, so quickly that I had no time to grab her. If she screamed, I could not hear it for the noise in the gym. Surely this was a bad dream.

Shakily, empty carrier in hand, I scrambled to the floor and under the risers. The baby lay face up bundled in a heavy blanket, silent for maybe five seconds, though it seemed an eternity before she let out a lusty cry, music to my ears.

"Oh, Jeanne," I cried. Weak with fear, I picked her up and held her close.

Pausing to calm myself, I emerged to search the gym for Frank. He stood several feet away, talking to George. Funny the things one notices at such moments—like George's red hair and beard and his short stature—sort of a return to normalcy to balance the crisis.

Sam, our young friend, saw me first and perhaps sensed my anxiety. "What's wrong, Clyta?" he asked.

Uncontrollable tremors shook me. "Could you get Frank please? Jeanne...fell."

Frank came running. "Is she all right?" he asked, his face pale and lined with worry.

I collapsed against him and struggled to talk over the reverberating noise of the gym. "Like a fool," the words came out between sobs, "I sat her next to me to take off my coat and...she...fell."

"Oh, honey, why did you..." Frank sighed. "I'm sorry, I didn't mean..." He put his arm around me, took Jeanne, and cuddled her a few moments, and the crying subsided. "Here, sit down."

"I don't think she's hurt, mostly scared, but I want to take her to the clinic," I said.

"Babies are tougher than they look," Sam offered. "Believe me, I'm the oldest of seven kids. Frank, is there any way I can help?"

"Thanks, I need to go with Clyta. It's just..."

"Why don't I take Clyta to the clinic?" Sam suggested. "If the doctor finds anything serious, I will come back for you immediately."

Frank looked skeptical.

I rested my hand on his arm and said, "The baby appears to be unhurt. We weren't far off the floor, and she is well padded. You shouldn't leave right now."

"Are you sure?"

"Yes. You stay."

"That might be best. Thanks, Sam." To me, he added, "Ruthie can stay with me."

When we arrived at the clinic, the nurse led me into a room. Jeanne howled in protest when undressed for the examination. First, Dr. Johnson scanned the pupils of her eyes with a small penlight. Then he carefully ran his hands over the surface of her head, neck, shoulders, and chest.

"How far did she fall?" he asked.

"We sat on the third row, so maybe three or four feet?"

"I've known babies to survive unharmed after a fall from a second-story window. She has no broken bones or bumps or bruises to the head, and there doesn't appear to be any internal injury. Her pupils are equal in size and normal. I think your baby's going to be fine."

Jeanne stopped crying and looked at the doctor as if to say, *Oh yeah, you sure about that?* She reached to grab his stethoscope.

We laughed, relieving some of the tension. Dr. Johnson grew quiet for a moment. "Mrs. Coder, you've had a rough go since moving to Cordova in January. You've had to adjust to a new baby and a new town." He paused a moment. "Taking care of this three-month-old baby and your other daughter is the most important job you have. Focus on the children and let your husband deal with school problems."

My eyes filled with tears. "I promise to do that doctor. I...I feel so guilty."

"No, no...the unpleasantness you've faced would have challenged anyone. Now," he added, "for the next twelve hours, you must wake the baby every two hours. If her pupils change in size or you cannot get her to awake, call me immediately. I don't think either is going to happen, but we have to be sure. Sorry, you won't get much sleep, but it's the only way to rule out concussion."

"Yes, Doctor, I'll do what you say, and thank you for your help and understanding."

*****

When Frank came home later that night, he looked beaten. He put his arms around me and held me close.

"Dr. Johnson checked the baby over thoroughly. She's fine, but I need to wake her every two hours to rule out concussion. Why don't you go to bed and get a few hours' sleep?"

"I'm so sorry about all this." He put his head in his hands. "Somehow we'll get through it."

My arms encircled him for a moment. "Sure we will. Go on to bed."

To silence negative thoughts, I asked God for His peace and felt my body relaxing, my mind calming. *Thank you, Lord*, I prayed, consoled with the assurance that God had wrapped his loving arms around Jeanne and protected her from the impact of a hard fall. I also prayed that any who might have seen what happened would be understanding and not give our family any more negative attention.

The rest of the night passed in a blur. The baby woke, nursed, slept, and woke, and I attempted to catch a few winks. By morning, we knew Jeanne had not been hurt by the fall. At five o'clock, she demanded breakfast with an insistent cry. I thanked God for his watch care over her and for his infinite mercy.

Bonds of Love

"Bear one another's burdens, and in this way, you will fulfill the law of Christ" (Galatians 6:2).

On Easter morning, I felt sad because Frank could not attend the church services with us. Warm memories came to mind of the long hours and hard work he had invested directing the *Messiah* chorus in Kenai on Easter Sunday 1976. Ironic that this morning he worked equally as hard in the local fish cannery to earn much needed extra money.

However, I chose happiness on this holy day. Victory and forgiveness is the stuff of Easter.

Ruthie's blue flowered dress, crocheted coat, and bonnet sent by Nana Nadine lifted my heart. At four months, Jeanne was comfortable in a pink sleeper. Dressed in a navy-blue suit, I headed to Community Baptist Church with my girls for the Sunday brunch and worship services. The women had gone all out, and the perfume of Easter lilies filled the fellowship hall. Their petals lent an ivory loveliness. Little girls dressed in pastel pinks, yellows, and lavenders looked like painted eggs; while the boys, handsome but uncomfortable, wore shirts with too-tight collars, ties, and dress pants that mamas had warned them not to get dirty.

My friend Kay took my hand. "The girls look so pretty this morning. How are you doing…really?" She gave me a concerned look.

"Good," I replied. "Life fits better today. Jeanne suffered no injuries from her fall, and Frank had a good day at school Friday. Oh, and Bud took the car and put in a new windshield."

"Great. Bud is one of our members who sees a need and meets it in a practical way. Well, duty calls. Looks like we need more coffee. See you later."

The congregation went out of their way to make me feel at ease, knowing of the assaults on our family during the past months. I loved them for it. We were a community of believers who bore each other's sorrows. Richard and Robert led us in an upbeat service of praise.

The pastors invited us to the parsonage at four o'clock for a supper of ham, deviled eggs, king crab casserole, chocolate cake, and fun. Frank joined us, tired and grateful for the friendly welcome and good food. The parsonage sat on a high hill. From their large picture window, you could see the bay with the late afternoon sun sparkling on the water.

We didn't press charges against the students who damaged the house and car because nothing was proven and there were no more attacks.

One day at the grocery store, a woman approached me to say, "I'm so sorry for your trouble. That isn't who we are." A new friend, Jan, often stopped by for coffee and offered to babysit so Frank and I could have a night out.

Elementary vocal music had always been Frank's strong point. The week before school was out, his elementary school choir sang a concert of folk tunes and concluded with the Alaska state song, "Alaska's Flag." Parents applauded the children and thanked Frank for his efforts. Their praise boosted his morale. At graduation, Nancy and other faithful band students performed a few numbers before the graduates received their diplomas. Things were looking up.

Chapter 15

Summer in Cordova

You have fixed all the bounds of the earth; you made summer and winter.
—Psalm 74:17

Spring brought fifteen hours of daylight—a tonic for the soul after six months of cold weather and long nights. Snow could still be seen on the distant Wrangell mountains, while lower elevations sprouted green grass, purple lupine, and brilliant goldenrod. Sunshine and warmer temperatures invited everyone outdoors to play and explore.

"Let's drive out the Copper River Highway," Frank said one Sunday in May.

"Great idea since it's a beautiful day. I'll pack a lunch. I'd like to see the bridge we've heard so much about. But why do Cordovans call it the Million Dollar Bridge?"

"One of the teachers told me that its proximity to the Miles Glacier made it hard to engineer…and the bridge wound up costing one-and-a-half million dollars."

"Why did they even need a bridge there?"

"The Kennecot copper mine used it to haul ore to market is what I've been told."

"Let's get the kids and our lunch in the car and see what was worth a million dollars," I replied.

Copper River Highway

We drove along the narrow Copper River Highway. It had no shoulders and traversed bridges over sloughs formed by the runoff of the Scott Glacier, thirteen miles northeast of Cordova. In the distance, we saw a bull moose, munching on willows, his bulbous nose thrust into the groves that lined the highway. Intent on his meal, he paid no attention to us.

Having read in *The Milepost* about the unfinished Copper River Highway, I knew it ran along the abandoned rails of the Northwestern Railway. Construction on the road to link Cordova to the Edgarton Highway and to interior Alaska started in 1945 but was never completed. The Good Friday earthquake in 1964 sounded the death knell, severely damaged its roadbeds and bridges, and dumped the north end of the Miles Glacier Bridge into the Copper River. The bridge was not repaired due to the prohibitive cost.

Dense alder grasses of dark green and Sitka spruce bordered the road, which turned to gravel twelve miles out of Cordova.

"How far does the road go?" I asked.

"About fifty miles according to the map. The road isn't maintained, but we'll go as far as we can. Let's stop here to eat lunch," Frank said as he pulled off into a wide expanse not far from a pond with room to park and have a picnic.

We sat on an old blanket to eat our ham and cheese sandwiches and drink sodas. Afterward, Ruthie ran off excess energy, while Frank and I relaxed with Jeanne on a blanket.

I must have dozed off when I heard Frank say, "Look, Ruthie, there's a moose standing in the pond." Frank pointed to the large creature. "Look," he said louder.

Ruthie, engrossed in chasing her ball, paid no attention to him. She never even looked to see the moose. Frank took a picture of her with the moose in the background, and just in case Mr. Moose might decide to come closer, we gathered blankets and kids into the car.

The Volvo jolted along the rutted highway. A few miles further, Ruthie shouted, "Big bird," from the backseat.

"A trumpeter swan, Ruthie," I said.

We watched the swan spread magnificent wings to glide gracefully across the pond and settle on the calm surface. A benediction of alabaster beauty on our relaxing day.

The washboard road rattled and bounced us on to Mile 49 where we found a bridge, brown with rust, with its far span fallen into the Copper River and overgrown with vegetation. I felt sorry for the old bridge; it had been forgotten, neglected, and left to the elements.

"Sure doesn't look worth a million dollars now," I commented. "Do you think the state will ever fix it?"

"Not unless they decide to connect the highway to the Edgarton. No, it's a bridge to nowhere."

One evening a few weeks later, we drove five miles out Whitshed Road to Hartney Bay to watch the spring migrations of shorebirds, mostly western sandpipers. From a distance, we heard the birds' piercing squeal punctuated by the staccato of thousands of flapping wings. A flurry of gray-brown and reddish feathers descended on the mudflats to feed on small crustaceans and mollusks. For miles the wall of birds dominated the shoreline, more birds than I have ever seen at one time.

Uncle Steve

In June, we welcomed Steve, Frank's younger brother, a twenty-year-old college student from California. He and Frank hoped to find employment in the St. Elias cannery for the summer. The day Steve arrived, I had intended to have a cup of coffee before he and Frank came from the airport. Somehow, I dropped the cup and coffee spilled on the carpet and spread in a large dark stain.

"Come on in, Steve," Frank said when they arrived. "Clyta's here somewhere," he added. They climbed the stairs, and Frank gave me an exasperated look and asked, "What are you doing?"

Embarrassed to be caught on my hands and knees with a bucket of cold water, scrubbing the carpet, I stood up, "Steve, great to see you…"

That's as far as I got because my foot hit the pail and knocked it over. Water drenched Steve's feet.

"Whew, that's cold water," Steve said, shaking his leg. Seeing my dismay, he added, "It's okay, I brought plenty of socks." We all had a good laugh.

Frank helped me clean up the mess, but for years the smell of stale coffee evoked memories of that day.

Our heated basement, equipped with an extra room, became Steve's summer home. It had no light or electric outlet, and Steve said it was pitch-black when he closed the door.

Poor Steve. The backpack with all his camping gear did not arrive with him. He had looked forward to a camping trip to Katmai National Park after he left us. The airlines told him not to worry, the backpack would probably arrive in a couple of days, but it didn't, and he called the airlines for several weeks, to no avail. I had little faith the backpack would be found. I remembered that Bruce, a visiting minister in Kenai, arrived in June and left in August without his luggage. He stood six feet four inches and spent the summer in clothes borrowed from one of our church members. I chose not to share this with Steve.

We needn't have worried about leisure time to show our guest the countryside. The week he arrived, before he could apply at St. Elias, the cannery workers went on a strike that lasted until a few days after July 4. The strike gave us plenty of time to become better acquainted with Steve. He tried his best to teach us to play backgammon, but the game remained a mystery to me.

Steve enjoyed the outdoors as much as we did. By June, the sun rose at four thirty, and didn't set till eleven. One day, we drove to a beach near Hartney Bay. It was about sixty degrees and overcast. Frank carried Jeanne in a carrier strapped to his back. Though the ocean in Alaska is much too cold for swimming, we burrowed our feet in the cool, squishy sand and let the glacial water wash over them. An endless variety of sea shells could be found on the beach—every shell was a treasure for Ruthie to plunk into her bucket. Wieners and marshmallows roasted over a campfire sure tasted good after a long walk.

On rainy days, Steve spent a lot of time reading *Green Eggs and Ham* by Dr. Seuss, to Ruthie who was two at the time. She loved to listen to his watch tick and to the rooster that crowed in one of the songs on his *Bonzo Dog Band* album. They became great friends that summer.

Jeanne was only six months old, and Uncle Steve wasn't sure what to do with her. One evening, he offered to keep Ruthie and Jeanne so we could celebrate our anniversary. Ruthie went to bed fairly easily, but when we returned, Jeanne was in her playpen slapping at wads of newspaper with ink-stained hands. Steve explained that when she started crying, he tried to give her a bottle but she wanted none of it. He put on the *Bonzo Dog Band* cassette and walked around bouncing her up and down. This worked for a short while until she began fussing again. The newspaper idea came to mind a few minutes before we returned to rescue him, and he was mighty glad to see us.

Helping with the children turned out to be good training for Steve. Today he and his wife, Angelica, have twin boys.

For our part, we had enjoyed an unusual anniversary celebration. Buckets of rain hit us sideways, blown by gale-like winds. A verse in a poem I wrote speaks of this:

> *Tonight each raindrop holds a memory of you...*
> *A rainy night in coastal Alaska,*
> *our anniversary, spent swimming,*
> *in the indoor pool*
> *to our car*
> *to the Reluctant Fisherman to eat.*

Streamlining the Trailer

Since the cannery workers strike dragged on, Frank enlisted Steve's help in rebuilding our travel trailer. The trailer was four feet wide, six feet long, and four feet high. He planned to replace the corrugated tin walls with wooden ones. The trailer was also to be lengthened to nine and one-half feet and widened to seven feet. To streamline the trailer, he would round the corners and the roof. A rounded roof would raise the height to six feet and one and one-half inches. Frank drew up plans, purchased materials at Cordova's well-equipped lumber and hardware store, and went to work. He was never deterred from action because he didn't know *exactly* how to do something.

For days, the men sawed and hammered, laughed and cursed in a cacophony of sound. Frank used the kerf-cut method to bend the wood for the roof. The strips of wood were about two inches wide and perhaps one-half-inch thick. To do this, he cut slots two-thirds deep, about one-half inch apart across the inside of the bend. He steamed the strips by boiling water in a large pan on the Coleman stove. Somehow, this worked, and he hammered the ends of the strips to the sides of the trailer, gluing each strip to the next one, then he covered the entire area with a veneer.

Steve had not been taught carpentry or anything mechanical because his father (Frank's stepfather) hired workmen for household repairs and mechanics to fix family vehicles. If his father wanted a travel trailer, he bought one. Frank's do-it-yourself projects amazed Steve, and he became a willing assistant. He told me later that he learned more about carpentry from Frank that summer than he ever had before or since and was grateful for the experience.

When the St. Elias Cannery strike ended the second week in July, Frank and Steve went to work there. They worked twelve to fourteen-hour shifts, dumping food products into a hopper or on a sorting table or conveyor. Or they fed products into processing equipment to be washed, peeled, cored, and pitted. The equipment also sliced and cooked the fish. All the tasks were wet, dirty, and smelly, and when Frank and Steve came home from the cannery late at night, the basement's outside entrance and shower came in handy.

When the men worked late into the evening, I took the girls and went to the Community Baptist parsonage where the co-pastors Richard Harding and Robert Varnum and their wives opened their home to lonely souls. A variety of people, young and old, gathered there to play cards and board games, drink coffee, and discuss the fishing season. I have warm memories of those times.

Steve earned enough money working in the cannery for his trip home and a camping trip to Katmai National Park. Katmai is located on the northern tip of the Alaska Peninsula, northwest of Kodiak Island. His backpack finally caught up with him at Kodiak, but he had to spend two days hanging around the post office before he got it.

Katmai is a volcanically devastated region surrounding Mount Katmai and the Valley of Ten Thousand Smokes. A large population of bears live in the park and feed on salmon from the rivers. A postcard from Steve told us, "Today a grizzly passed close to my tent. The ranger had told us to whistle or make noise to frighten a bear away. I never was much of a whistler, and when I saw that bear, I froze and couldn't have whistled even if I'd tried."

He must have unfrozen, though, because we received a picture of the grizzly.

*****

Our time in Cordova was coming to an end. Frank's cannery earnings paid for a flight to Glennallen, Alaska for a job interview. True to his word, his former mentor, George Wiese, gave him a good recommendation, as did fellow teachers in Cordova. He got a position teaching music, K-12, in Glennallen, a small interior town 189 miles east of Anchorage. Our Cordova journey came full circle when we boarded the Alaska ferry to Valdez toward the end of August.

We were happy that Frank would have another chance to teach, but sad to leave the warm fellowship of Community Baptist Church and our friends Richard and Susan Harding. The prospects of another move to start over in a new place after only seven months might have defeated us. We considered each Alaska experience an opportunity to see more of that wild, beautiful country we had come to love.

Lyrics from the song, "How Can I Keep from Singing" voiced my sentiments:

My life flows on in endless song, above earth's lamentations,
I hear the sweet, though far-off hymn that hails a new creation;
Above the tumult and the strife I hear the music ringing;
It finds an echo in my soul—How can I keep from singing?

Chapter 16

New in Town—Again

Jesus said to him, If it is my will that he remain until I come, what is that to you? Follow me.
—*John 21:22*

Introduction to Glennallen

On our first Sunday in Alaska in 1975, we drove through the community of Glennallen and listened to a program of hymns on the radio.

"Look." I pointed to the sign on a brownstone building and read, "K-C-A-M.

That was our introduction to Glennallen, Alaska, a town about 180 miles northeast of Anchorage. Now, on a morning in August of 1979, four years later, we boarded the Alaska Ferry in Cordova to move there.

*****

The weather smiled on us with shirt-sleeve temperatures—sixty-five degrees and sunny. Passengers included more tourists than locals. Topside, we heard a cacophony of compliments paid to the majestic mountain scenery, combined with the squeals of children at play and the frequent complaints of bored teenagers.

Ruthie, our three-year-old, had exhausted herself and fallen asleep. Baby Jeanne napped peacefully, while Frank and I took advantage of the lull with a cup of coffee.

"I would be excited if I were not so tired from packing, goodbye parties, and chasing the kids," I said.

"Maybe we won't have to move again for a while," Frank said. "Moving has become a familiar and exhausting occupation."

About one o'clock the ferry arrived at Valdez, the southern terminus of the Richardson Highway and the trans-Alaska oil pipeline. In 1964, the Good Friday Earthquake had caused massive underwater landslides that destroyed the wharf, killing thirty-three people. The Army Corps of Engineers determined the town should be relocated on Port Valdez, an estuary off Valdez Arm on Prince William Sound.

"I can see why Valdez is sometimes called Little Switzerland," I said, when we came into port. The Chugach mountains looked like giant snow-clad sentinels guarding the harbor.

The two-hour drive to Glennallen took more than three hours because we pulled a trailer packed with our belongings and stopped two or three times to see to the needs of the children. While Frank drove, I skimmed through information on Glennallen sent to us by the school superintendent.

"About half of the people are connected in some way with the Central Alaska Mission. It operates a radio station, Faith Hospital, and staffs the Bible College and Community Bible Church."

We learned later that the Reverend Vincent Joy and his wife, Becky, fundamentalist missionaries, founded the mission in 1953 to serve people in the Valdez-Cordova census district.

Frank turned his attention back to the road, and I navigated. Detours caused by the inevitable summer road construction slowed us down. The countryside in that part of Alaska consisted of expansive flatlands dotted by shrubs such as serviceberry, juniper, and wild rose bushes amid tamarack, white spruce, and paper birch trees. Towering high in the background were the snow-capped Wrangell mountains. We followed the directions sent to us by Keith Swenson*, the superintendent of schools, and pulled up in front of his house around four thirty that afternoon.

This was Keith's first year in Glennallen also. He and his family had come from a coastal village not far from Nome and about one thousand miles due west of Fairbanks.

Keith and Marilyn welcomed us into their home and introduced us to Doug, the new school counselor who had recently moved to Glennallen from Kansas City. While we ate a simple meal prepared by Marilyn, Keith told us more about the town.

(*Names in this chapter have been changed.)

"About one thousand people live here. The mission is staffed by volunteers who sign on for two years."

"What about the residents?" I asked.

"There's the teaching staff, of course. And National Park Service employees, oil pipeline workers and their families. Many of them are members of the church and are influenced by the mission's conservative thinking."

The rest of the townsfolk, we soon learned, were typical independent Alaskans who didn't want to be bothered with organized anything. Thus, Glennallen was a somewhat polarized community. Like oil and water, the two halves didn't mix.

New Digs

After dinner, Keith told us about a mobile home for rent at a reasonable price. He phoned the owner and manager of the Pine Tree Trailer Park. Her daughter told him she was at a church meeting and would be home shortly and suggested we come right over. When we arrived, a young woman dressed in jeans and a T-shirt greeted us with a smile.

"Hi. I'm Cindy, come on in." She showed us to a combination living room and office. "Mom should be home soon," she said and disappeared.

We sat on an old sofa and waited and waited. Frank riffled through a dog-eared copy of *The Alaska Sportsman*, and I read *Green Eggs and Ham* to Ruthie a couple of times. Ten o'clock rolled around with no sign of the woman. Jeanne began crying, and I fed her. Ruthie fell asleep, and Frank and I tried not to nod off—our day had begun about five o'clock that morning.

Frank announced impatiently, "If she doesn't come soon, we're going to get a motel room."

"A motel room?" I repeated. "Remember where you are. Did you *see* a motel anywhere?"

At that, he laughed. "Right."

About that time, a large woman walked in. "Hello, I'm Joanne Miller. I'm so sorry you have had to wait. Had a late meeting at the church and the phone wasn't working, so my daughter couldn't call me." Her stern face and gray-streaked hair pulled back in a tight bun gave her an air of authority.

She showed us a double-wide mobile home, approximately twenty-four by seventy feet and in fair shape. The combination living room, dining room, and kitchen had wide, louvered windows on three sides, a nice feature in a land where the winter sun shines only four to six hours a day. Faded curtains, torn in several places, and a burnt-orange shag carpet completed the sparse décor. One fairly large bedroom, two smaller ones, all with walnut paneling, composed the remainder of the mobile home. It had no washer or dryer and had one tiny bathroom. Because it was the only available housing in town, we rented it.

When we finally got our family into the mobile home about eleven o'clock, Frank threw together the crib for Jeanne, and the rest of us slept in sleeping bags on the floor.

The next evening, we were exhausted from carrying housewares and furniture inside from the trailer and caring for two active children. In addition, Frank had been in two meetings with the principal. For supper, we ate canned pork and beans and sandwiches made with our last pieces of bread.

To our surprise, we heard a knock at the door, and when Frank answered it, he found a smiling young couple with a baby girl and a boy about Ruthie's age.

"I'm Richard and this is my wife, Jackie," the young man said.

"We wanted to come by to bring you some sourdough bread and welcome you to Glennallen," Jackie added.

"Well, come right in," Frank said.

After they stepped inside and sat down, I held the bread to my nose and said, "Hmm, smells good, and you brought it at a perfect time because we finished our last loaf for supper. Thanks."

Frank looked at the little boy. "What are the children's names?"

"This is Sheldon. He's three," Richard said.

"Great! The same age as our daughter." I turned and said, "Ruthie, here's someone for you to play with." This was her cue to duck behind her dad.

"And this is Chandelle." Jackie smiled down at the baby who looked to be about nine months.

Before long, we were laughing and talking like old friends, and Ruthie and Sheldon were playing together in the bedroom. We learned that Richard and Jackie hailed from Canada and were volunteers at the Central Alaska Mission where Richard piloted the mission plane. Jackie, like me, was a homemaker.

Richard noticed a record album in the front of a box. "You like Bach played on the harpsichord?"

Frank's face lit up like Times Square at Christmas, and he spoke in a crescendo. "Yes, yes. Bach is my favorite composer, and especially on the harpsichord."

"You'll have to come over and see the harpsichord I built," Richard said.

"Oh, I would love to…just tell me when."

"Do you play also?" I asked Jackie.

"The piano," she replied.

About that time, the babies started fussing, and we heard Ruthie yell, "No, no!" It seems Sheldon's tall tower of blocks had crashed onto an empty stroller where her imaginary friend, "Coo," sat.

"Sounds like it's time for us to go," Jackie said.

We agreed to get together again when Richard returned from a trip to Southeast Alaska. In the months ahead, we became good friends.

In the yard one day, I met our next-door neighbor, Jenny Ross, and her cute toddler, Erin. Jenny and her husband hailed from Toronto and volunteered at the mission. She suggested Ruthie and Jeanne come over to play with Erin for a while so I could accomplish more unpacking.

The children had great fun, and we decided on a reciprocal agreement whereby I would keep Erin on Thursday morning during Jenny's Bible study and she would keep Ruthie and Jeanne when I needed a sitter. When school started, I volunteered to watch the choir accompanist's ten-month-old baby. I couldn't help Frank by playing the piano, but I could offer child care.

Toward the end of the week, I could not put off the dreaded trip to the laundromat. Even without children, I had always thought laundromats an ordeal and with two children, well, climbing a mountain might be easier. A major part of the hassle was getting the clothes and children into the car and out of the car into the laundromat and back into the car to go home. Exhausted, I still had to unload the car and get children and clean clothes into the house.

The washers and dryers cost seventy-five cents a load, and often they did not function properly. On the other hand, once inside, Ruthie had great fun pushing the laundry carts and running around the large room.

"I really don't understand how going to the laundromat can be as hard as you say," Frank said one evening when I bemoaned my fate.

All right, buddy, just wait! The next wash day, you're going to help.

His day to help came on a Saturday a couple of weeks later. "Frank, I'm feeling a little off today and the girls are out of clean clothes. Could you please help me do the laundry?" I asked.

"Sure, I'll go." He paused. "If you're positive it can't wait until Monday."

"It can't," I replied.

After we had strapped Ruthie and Jeanne in their car seats and made two trips to carry the laundry, Ruthie insisted she needed to go to the bathroom. Back in the house, she and I went. When we returned, Frank said, "Guess who needs to be changed now?"

My nose told me who, and into the house I went with Jeanne. About fifteen minutes, later we arrived at the laundromat, which was much busier than usual.

To make a long story short, two of the machines were not working, and it took us four hours to do laundry that day. Frank never questioned my frustration again.

*****

Life for me settled into a routine of domestic responsibilities: babysitting, attending a weekly ladies' Bible study, and helping with Awana meetings, an organization for elementary age girls. In October, I also began a program to improve my writing that was suggested by the book *How to Write, Speak and Think More Effectively*. I had received the book at the Sunday school writers conference two years earlier. The assignment: each day write a five-hundred-word letter to someone I knew well. The letters were to be written as if I were having a conversation with the person. They could be on any topic. Mother was the chosen recipient for my letters about our life in Alaska. When I wrote and asked her, she answered, "I would love to receive your letters and I'll do my best to make helpful comments." She kept the letters, and they tell a great deal of my Glennallen story.

First, I will skip ahead to a letter which gives a physical description of Glennallen.

> December 11, 1979
>
> In this letter, I will describe a short trip to the Community Bible Church. As I drive from our mobile home, I see other mobile homes of various sizes and shapes...some with skirting, some without, fenced and unfenced. There is no housing code in Glennallen because there is no organized city government.
>
> The only bank is in front of the court to the highway. It is brown and beige with huge windows all around.

Directly across the highway from us is the Tastee Freeze. It's a hub of activity—the local hamburger joint you might say. The Freeze is the only place in town you can get a meal for a family of four for under ten dollars. They stay open all year round, winter too. When we told people in Cordova we were moving here, they would brighten up and say, "Glennallen has a Tastee Freeze." I never thought having a Tastee Freeze in a town would be such a novelty.

Next, I pass a small clothing and gift shop called Santa's Clothing Store. The building looks ordinary but the owner, Mrs. Olsen, is a little different. She's an older lady who moves very slowly and mumbles, to herself and everyone else. Her store doesn't open until noon----a fact which I keep forgetting. Typical Alaska. Independent shop owners tend to keep hours to suit their lifestyle.

This is true of the Cracker Barrel Country Store also. It is a small general store. They have a little of everything but not a surplus of anything. Prices are high, even with the 15% discount teachers get. Before pipeline days, their prices were 100% higher than stores in Anchorage. The nostalgia of the place almost makes up for the high prices. Ceilings and walls are covered with old photos of Wiley Post and Will Rogers and movie stars like Judy Garland, also, memorabilia of early Alaska.

Moving on down the road, I see the Faith Hospital, a small green building. It is an eight-bed hospital with an outpatient clinic. Because it is funded in part by the Central Alaska Mission, the fees are unbelievably low. When recently have you paid $5 for an office call?

I have now arrived at Community Bible Church, a log cabin building, rustic and quaint.

Every small-town USA has its quirks, and Glennallen was no exception. Frank realized the mission's influence on the local scene early in the game when he was told the high school band could not play Glenn Miller's "In the Mood"—too racy. We enjoyed a good laugh, and since Frank had a lot of Sousa marches or classical pieces to choose from, he didn't mind.

Another sign of the conservative influence was the low-key observance of Halloween—no sign of witches, goblins, or ghouls, only tasteful costumes, which were mostly homemade like they were before all holidays became so commercialized. To make Ruthie's clown costume, I took an old red maternity blouse and put ruffled sleeves on it, a bow, and a huge button front. She wore it over her snowsuit because even in October, the temperature hovered around zero and snow covered the ground. Frank took her to a few pre-arranged homes of friends.

*****

One letter to Mother tells of a shopping trip to Anchorage.

> November 2, 1979
>
> Whew! It's 10:30 at night and I think I've got everything ready to go to Anchorage tomorrow... We haven't been to "the city" for over two years. Just think—a choice of grocery and department stores, several restaurants to choose from. I'm really excited.
>
> Anchorage is about 150 miles from Glennallen, but we've realized that in order to save any money on groceries and other needs, it's necessary to drive to Anchorage every six weeks. We've been told that before the pipeline, Glennallen had no reasonably priced shopping. Members of the teachers' association now get

a ten percent discount at one local store which about equals the Anchorage shelf prices, but not the "specials." The other store is way too high. Everyone says what you save on groceries will pay for the gas. We are skeptical, with the price of gas here being over two dollars a gallon.

Saturday dawned bright and clear. There was snow on the ground, but the roads were in good shape. Parts of the countryside we drove through were completely white—ground, trees, bushes, everything—an icy wonderland. It was beautiful.

We stopped for pie and coffee at a lodge halfway between Glennallen and Anchorage. Eating there brought back memories. We ate there our first day in Alaska, on the way to Kenai, two churches and two babies ago. Another incident to remind us that things never stay the same.

Anchorage was a busy place on Saturday, people everywhere. I'm afraid that shopping when I have to but don't have a lot of time, is not my favorite thing, especially with a baby ten-month-old baby and a three-year-old in tow. We had finished with two grocery stores, and I needed to stop at a drugstore. Frank stayed in the car with the children.

When I came out, I saw what I thought was our car, but the hood was up and two men were bending over it. I said to myself, "That looks like our Volvo, but we're not having car trouble." On I went only to realize that it was our car. Not surprising, because the Volvo seems unable to go over a week without having some problem. The battery was low, and some guy was jumping it, but to no avail, so Frank went to call our friend Bill Canary who drove across town with some battery cables. When he attached them, the car started.

Frank talked with Bill a few moments, and when he got in the car, told me that Bill and Pat were leaving Alaska this week. I didn't know whether to cry over that or over the dumb car. Bill was the Alaska Baptist Music Director until last summer when he resigned. There was quite a shake up in the convention, and I guess he no longer wanted to be involved. He and Pat helped us so much when Frank had problems in Kenai and Fairbanks. We came to love them and hated to see them go. It's funny how situations change and even seem to reverse themselves.

A big full moon shone on us all the way home that evening—so beautiful.

I scribbled this poem on a sheet of paper and claimed it for the days ahead:

> Moon over Alaska
> light our way home.
> Remind us of God's
> watch care,
> His eye of counsel
> to guide us.

*****

CHAPTER 17

Holidays in Glennallen

The Lord reigns; let the earth rejoice;
—*Psalms 97:1a(KJV)*

Writing letters to Mother encouraged me to describe the environment and culture of a small town in interior Alaska—the people, the local politics, and how Frank and I related to them. Holidays for her meant being with family, while ours were spent with friends who had become like family.

In the next letters, I tell how we celebrated Thanksgiving, Christmas, and New Year's Eve.

> November 25, 1979
> Thanksgiving Day brought friends from Fairbanks, Linda and Owen Fansler and their two children for lots of fellowship and fun. Darcie was four and Kevin, sixteen months. With four preschoolers between us, we had plenty of happy activity.
> Frank met them at the door when they arrived about two that afternoon. Kevin had become car sick just as they rolled into Glennallen. In typical Fansler fashion (They're a lot like us, that's why we get on so well.), Owen sat down with Kevin

and said, "Honey, you can clean up the mess in the car later, don't worry about it now,"

"Thanks a lot, Owen," Linda said, struggling to catch a recovered, wriggling Kevin. The good-natured kidding we always enjoyed with the Fanslers had begun. One of the secrets of our friendship is that none of us feels he has to put on a front.

Armed with paper towels and cleaning rags, Linda and I went out and cleaned the mess in the car. Back inside, we worked together to set the table, make giblet gravy, and pour drinks. The golden brown sixteen-pound bird I had baked looked yummy, if I do say so myself.

"Frank, carve some meat and put it in the oven to warm rather than heating the whole turkey," I suggested.

He carved for a few minutes then said, "I have an idea, why don't I put this meat I've carved back into the oven to warm, rather than trying to heat the whole bird."

I stared at him. "That's what I just said."

We all laughed. I'd foolishly given instructions while he and Owen were discussing Owen's new Plymouth Arrow.

We lined the food up "buffet style" as our small table couldn't hold the feast. In the center of the table, I put the cranberry sauce on a silver tray with an aqua bowl of carrot/raisin salad. Our dinner included cornbread dressing, Pilgrim Pumpkin Pie (a vegetable dish with parsley, onions and soy sauce in it) and green bean casserole. After we prayed, I jokingly said, "Do you think we'll have enough?"

Later, kids fed, we adults sipped coffee and caught up on family happenings. It didn't take long for the kids to drag all of the toys down the hall, through the kitchen and into the living room. Soon our house looked really lived in.

Our turkey day was topped off with dessert at the church, along with a Walt Disney movie, *The Snowball Express*. Saturday night we got a sitter and had an evening out with our friends, their treat. On the drive home, we marveled at a splendid view of the Aurora, all multi-shades of green splashing the night sky. I love Alaska.

We hated to see Owen and Linda leave and promised to visit them in Fairbanks after Christmas.

Changes

On the second week in December, we decided to move to the mobile home next door that our neighbors had recently vacated.

We rented the current mobile home from the owner of the trailer park, and I questioned how she might view the move. One evening, I brought up the subject with Frank.

"Will she be angry with us for moving in winter when she might not be able to find another renter?"

"I hope not, but we have to consider our needs. The cost to heat this one really bites into my salary. The smaller trailer has a washer and dryer—no more laundromat."

"You've got a point. I'm going to pray the trailer doesn't sit empty too long."

In answer to my prayer, an oil-pipeline worker rented it in a matter of days.

The move solved some of our domestic problems and caused new ones. Transporting boxes from our mobile home to the one next door took longer because a person must move slower when it's twenty below zero. December is one of the busiest months for a music teacher, and Frank did not take time to wrap the exposed plumbing. When the temperature dipped even lower, our pipes froze and burst, causing a huge mess. Frank crawled under the house with a blow dryer on an extension cord and managed to thaw the pipe and wrap it sufficiently so that it would not burst again. Then he borrowed a wet vac to soak up the water and put sheeting over the wet carpet until it dried, which took a few weeks.

When we went to Anchorage in November, our funds were low and we could not buy Christmas gifts. Sears and Roebuck came to the rescue. We ordered each of the children a toy, and Frank and I chose two or three low-cost items and marked them. Frank chose a gift for me from one of them, and I chose one for him, and since neither of us knew exactly what gift the other would choose, we could still be surprised on Christmas morning.

Christmas is a celebration of Christ's birth, and that was our focus. We enjoyed our recordings of Handel's *Messiah,* the Christmas music on the radio, and the special programs at church.

The following letter describes our Christmas and New Years' Eve celebrations.

> December 25, 1979
>
> Tonight, I will recap our Christmas for you.
>
> Because this is the first year Ruthie has expressed interest in the Christmas celebration and the first year the girls could react to each other, it has been a special day for all of us. Though it is minus twenty-five degrees outside, our hearts have been warmed.
>
> We were invited over to a neighbors' home for dinner. Our hostess wouldn't let me bring much since our oven is on the blink. All the adults there were teachers, and school was a main topic.
>
> All in all, we had an enjoyable day. I thank God for my family, both here and far away. There's always a sadness when I think of all of you, but I've accepted that my home is with my husband and children. Thank you so much for

the money you and grandmother sent. You're both such a blessing to us.

The day after Christmas, we drove to Fairbanks to visit the Fansler's and shop.

Before we left, I asked Frank, "Have you got your glasses, keys, and billfold?"

"Yes. Yes, and yes," he replied. But when he reached for his billfold to pay for our pie and coffee two hours later—no wallet. He groaned. "I forgot to get it out of my other pants."

I must confess that I had also forgotten to wear my boots. Fortunately, the weather had warmed up to ten degrees above zero.

To make a long story short and show you what good friends the Fanslers are, they loaned us three hundred dollars to do our shopping and take Jeanne to the doctor. We laughed and talked and played cards, while the kids enjoyed playing together. Too soon it was time to go home. We sent Owen a check when we returned to Glennallen.

*****

January 2, 1980

What do you do on New Year's Eve in Alaska when the thermometer reads minus 40 degrees? You ignore the thermometer and your better judgement, and you go somewhere to celebrate like everyone in the lower forty-eight does. That's what we did anyway. Friends of ours in Copper Center, about ten miles from here, invited us to their home for a movie and goodies. We packed Jeanne and Ruthie into the car, bundled in snowsuits, made sure we had plenty of warm clothes and blankets, some finger food, and headed out. Frank had plugged in the engine a couple of hours before and the car started right up.

You might wonder what the countryside looks like at minus forty degrees. Actually, that's often when winter is most beautiful. It was a clear night, with a huge full moon, surrounded by a circle. The stars shone so large, you could almost pick one from the sky. Patches of ice fog hung low here and there along the highway. Ice Fog is eerie. I saw what looked like a blanket over my head. I blinked and it was gone.

When we arrived at the Finch's log cabin home—they built it themselves—we asked if this was the place where all those crazy people were who get out in minus forty-degree weather. We joined them upstairs in the family room to watch *Those Magnificent Men in Their Jaunty Jalopies*. Frank was the projectionist. The girls played happily with the other dozen or so children. Between movies we went downstairs and ate, plenty of goodies and hot tea and coffee. Also, during the break, everyone went out to start the cars for a few minutes.

We bid goodbye to 1979, a roller-coaster year of joy and pain and change, and wondered what 1980 would bring.

Chapter 18

The Inside Story

I will instruct you and teach you the way you should go.
—Psalm 32:8

The winter of 1980 brought temperatures that dipped between minus thirty and minus forty degrees—the coldest we had yet experienced in our five years in Alaska. Under clear blue skies, ice formed stalactites on buildings, trees, and bushes. Anyone who ventured outdoors had to cover the mouth with a scarf to warm the air before it entered the lungs. This was especially important for infants and small children. Uncovered skin surfaces can be frostbitten within minutes. Layered clothing provided greater warmth—thermal underwear, a sweater or sweat shirt, and woolen pants and a hooded parka with insulated mittens and boots could save your life. The upside—the air outside felt warm when the thermometer climbed above zero again after two weeks of temperatures below minus thirty.

Winter's long hours of darkness, isolation, and harsh temperatures seldom bothered me—but Frank became more irritable and restless—always happy when the days grew longer.

We often couldn't get outside and sought entertainment inside. Every afternoon at four o'clock, we tuned in to an episode of *Lum and Abner* on the radio. To some that may sound dull, but we enjoyed the slower pace of life. Radio transported us back to our childhood. This would be a good topic for a letter to Mother, I decided.

January 6, 1980

The local radio station plays Lum and Abner each afternoon. Frank had listened to the show with his dad in the early '50s. Here is the plot of one show:

The scene takes place at the Jot 'em down store where the two gentlemen are discussing Squire Skimp's recent offer to buy in as a third partner in the "movie house" they planned to open in Pine Ridge, Arkansas.

Lum: I didn't sleep a wink thinkin' about that movie house.

Abner: Oh yeah! We gotta get 'er open before squire finds a way to open one.

Lum: He'll find a way too. Ever time we ever done business with 'im, we got the fuzzy end of the lollypop for sure.

Abner: Huh? What's that? I don't recollect squire ever givin' us a lollypop at all.

Lum: No, Abner, I don't mean he actually give us one…never mind. Anyway, he's sure got our hands tied.

Abner: Our hands tied? My hands ain't tied, Lum. Are your'n?

Lum: Dab nab it, Abner, I don't mean he has our hands tied with rope—

Abner: What, then?

Lum: I mean he's got us so by the collar, we cain't turn around.

Abner: Now, Lum, nobody's got aholt of my collar, ner yourn neither.

Lum: Abner, cain't you understand nuthin!

And, so on. Pretty tame stuff, but that's how it was.

Our entertainments were simple, and even local meetings provided a diversion. For instance, the meetings of the Glennallen Library Committee rivaled any situation comedy.

> January 10, 1980
>
> To give you more local color, I'll describe a library meeting in November.
>
> Glennallen has no city government and no library funds, and the library has to be supported by donations. Since we use the library, I decided to attend the meeting. Charlotte Highbargain, the library board president, greeted my friend Mary and me, and soon others trickled in, until there were eight of us.
>
> "So happy to have two newcomers, Mrs. Coder and Mrs. Hofstedder. We're pretty informal here, so feel free to say whatever you want. We need some suggestions about how to get more people to use and support the library," Charlotte said.
>
> She explained that three months ago, they were able to hire a librarian when they got a grant from the state. Until then, funds came from donations and often she and Mary, the treasurer, had to pay for items out of their pockets. Someone had also suggested they rent out a small room in the building, but unfortunately, partly due to the fact that the space has no bathroom, the only taker was the Parks Department—and that made some people angry.
>
> "Many in Glennallen don't like the US Forest and Parks Department," Charlotte said. "People feel the government is attempting to tie up all the land so that no hunting, fishing, or mining can be done on it. Mary and I have even been threatened."

I had seen the signs in the windows of some businesses that read, "We will not serve employees of the parks department."

"My husband and I want to support the library," I said. But we do feel the hours might need to be extended to more evenings. I mean, most people are working or in school between 2:00 and 4:00 in the afternoon and [they] sometimes might not be able to come on Thursday nights or Saturday."

"I've heard several complaints about the hours, too," Mary said.

"And I've come by, and no one was here," Janice said. "How are the hours publicized?"

Charlotte explained that announcements had been on the radio, but not recently.

Then she repeated what Mrs. Olsen*, the owner of Santa's Gift Shop had just mumbled. "Mrs. Olsen has it posted in her store."

Mary looked at me and rolled her eyes. We both knew that Mrs. Olsen's "posted hours"— in crayon, no less—were about as legible as her voice was audible.

"I've worked in libraries in West Virginia, and there are lots of ways you can publicize a library," offered Janice. "Somebody could write an article for the paper and announce it on the radio's community calendar. Or, have someone write regular book reviews, have a story hour for children and read a story on the radio."

I volunteered to write book reviews, at the same time reminding myself not to take any more jobs.

The librarian finally arrived, and we rehashed the library hours. Mrs. Hofstedder suggested we change the evening hours from

Thursday to Tuesday, as she and many others had to bring daughters to ballet and had no place to wait for them. We finally decided the library would be open Tuesday, 5-9; Thursday through Saturday, 2-6.

That settled, Charlotte announced, "Ladies, we need to elect new officers." "My husband has threatened to leave me if I don't shed some responsibilities. Any volunteers?"

"I pass. My husband said I could come tonight only if I didn't take any jobs," Margaret said.

Somehow, we elected new officers. Janice accepted president, but she's moved back to Virginia since then. The rest of us agreed to be on the "board of directors." So far, we haven't done anything. At ten p.m., the three-hour meeting finally ended.

The next letter tells of a humorous experience of one of the teachers.

(*The names of the shop owner and those of the teachers and administrators at the school have been changed.)

February 20, 1980

Since Frank has been teaching, I've learned a lot about teachers. Like doctors, and everyone else, they are human and have foibles. Sometimes they can be petty with one another. And sometimes they act juvenile because they're around children and teenagers so much. Last week at faculty meeting, Frank said there was a couple sitting in a truck, necking in full view of the meeting room. One teacher saw them and went to the window for a look-see. Soon several other teachers were crowded around the window watching.

Another incident a teacher told me about is an example of the pecking order of administration and teachers. My friend, a woman who teaches English, had to go to a conference in Anchorage with two teachers and the assistant superintendent, all of them but her, male. The men decided to leave at five in order to get there for the nine-o'clock-morning session. Mrs. Jenkins* hates to do anything any earlier than eight. But, being outnumbered, she agreed. Her first irritation was when they stopped at a lodge to eat breakfast. "I've already had breakfast," she said.

"Well, you can just have coffee," one of the men commented.

That irritated her because she had gotten up earlier than she would have to eat breakfast.

Then, they were on an expense account, so it was agreed there would be no "personal shopping time." Everyone seemed to nod assent to that.

Before the evening meal, the four conferees were told they had $20 between them for food.

"You can eat enough on five dollars," Dr. Cantner, the assistant superintendent, said. (Actually, you rarely find a meal for $5 in Alaska.) One man said he was hungrier than that and paid for his own.

The final blow came when they stopped to let Dr. Cantner out at his home. He opened the trunk and got out several packages he had bought in Anchorage. No shopping, remember. Now wouldn't you think professional men and women would be a little more mature?

The letter above was the last one I wrote to Mother as part of the exercises to improve my writing. Unfortunately, I lost the letters

Mother wrote in reply. I wish I had continued writing daily letters the rest of our years in Alaska.

*****

All in all, the teaching year went pretty well for Frank though some of the students grumbled when he grouped them differently in band and choir. However, his teaching style was more formal than the former teacher, and he had a more abrupt way of dealing with students and parents. He felt intense pressure to succeed since his confidence had taken a beating in the years prior to Glennallen. It may be too that Superintendent Swenson also felt pressured to succeed in his first year and did not support his teachers when parents criticized. Also, our former landlady had a lot of influence on the school board.

One morning, Frank had forgotten a sheet of music and returned home looking grim.

"What's wrong?" I asked.

"Keith called me into his office. He said several parents had come to him to complain that their kids don't like the way I teach and wanted to drop band and that the school board would be convening to discuss it with him."

Without giving me a chance to say anything, he picked up the sheet music and said, "I need to get back," and left, slamming the door.

I called my friend Jackie and over the phone my voice choked mid-sentence, and Jackie suggested I come over.

Once inside her house, she led Ruthie to play with Sheldon while we talked.

She was silent for a few minutes, then suggested, "Maybe Frank could meet with the parents to explain his teaching policies and they could come to agreement on some issues."

"Yes, that would probably help" Previously, I had shared with Jackie the problems in Fairbanks and Cordova. "He just can't lose this job…"

Jackie brought me a cup of spiced tea and a piece of gingerbread. "Here, this will warm you."

When we finished eating, we prayed together, asking God to help Frank and guide him in his teaching and in talking with parents and the school board.

Church members and the women at the Bible study tried to understand. Persons connected with the mission couldn't afford to take sides, and that sometimes caused them to seem unfriendly.

The day the superintendent told him his contract would not be renewed, Frank came into the house and dropped into a chair. "Two failures in a row. No one's going to give me another teaching position," he said.

Sitting next to him, I covered his hand with mine, but he shrugged me away. "Sorry, but I need to be alone for a while."

The children were playing happily in their room. With a leaden heart, I went to prepare dinner.

Over the years, one thing has become clear to me: sometimes the most important contribution a caring friend can make is to pray and be silent. Often the words "I understand," or even "God will take care of you" are shallow and trite to one who feels betrayed. When Marilyn, the principal's wife, came by one afternoon with her mother who was visiting from Minnesota, I put on a gracious smile and served them spiced tea.

We chatted about our children, the weather, church activities, circling around the real topic that I suspected Marilyn wanted to bring forward. Finally, she said, "I'm sorry about what has happened, and I understand how you must feel."

No, you don't understand, I thought.

She paused for a moment, "Keith said you and Frank have considered missionary work for the Baptist convention. Perhaps that might be a next step."

Harsh words came to mind, instead I said, "When we left seminary in December of 1973, we wanted to be missionaries in South America but needed two years of successful service in the States first. The convention will not hire couples over thirty-two years of age, nor will they hire someone out of an unsuccessful situation." My voice had shrunk to almost a whisper on the last sentence.

Marilyn and her mother were silent, and after a few more uncomfortable minutes, took their leave.

Faith in *the fact* of God's love was the only thing that kept us going during those dark days. We certainly did not *feel* the joy of our faith much of the time. I began to wonder about the inability of Christian people to see another's pain, to be able to forgive such trivial mistakes. Sometimes, it was all I could do to keep from judging everyone harshly and feeling sorry for myself, withdrawing and becoming bitter. In fact, I did stop attending Bible study; and on Sunday morning, we often drove to a Baptist mission church in Kenny Lake, Alaska, where we felt more comfortable.

True friends like Richard and Jackie listened without judging or offering unwanted advice.

*****

Frank had been practicing the Easter portion of Handel's *Messiah* with an adult community chorus, which gave him a needed focus. Nothing stirred Frank's heart and emotions like his beloved classical music. For us, to sing *Messiah* was a worship experience. The Glennallen chorus was smaller than the one in Kenai, but more of the singers read music and had trained voices.

I had a babysitter for Ruthie and Jeanne during most of the practices, but occasionally we had to take them with us. I remember watching Ruthie push Jeanne around the room in the stroller crooning "all we like sheep have gone astray-ay-ay-ay" at the top of her voice.

In spite of a few bumps and hitches along the way, our chorus performed *Messiah* on Easter Sunday afternoon to a small audience. The music blessed us all and lifted our spirits during this difficult time.

Journaling and writing stories helped me to focus on something other than our immediate problems. We didn't have much time to dwell on the hurts because we had decided that, no matter what happened in Glennallen, we were going "outside" to California, Arkansas, and Oklahoma to visit family. We had not seen family in over three years, and no one had seen Jeanne, who was eighteen months old by then. Frank also planned to take a course, Assertive Discipline, in Pomona, California, about fifty miles from Woodland Hills where his mother lived.

Before we could travel, Frank needed to have surgery for a double hernia. He was admitted to the local Faith Hospital for hernia repair on May 19. I had a few qualms when he told me he chose to have the surgery there rather than go to Anchorage to a larger hospital. As it turned out, that was an excellent choice. Dr. Jim Pinneno worked wonders, and Mrs. Pinneno, the nurse, gave Frank excellent care. Thanks to them, he spent only three days in the hospital and a week later was able to resume normal activities. Since then, more than one of our male friends has been amazed when Frank shared his story. They had a much longer recovery after the same surgery.

*****

We had decided that I would go to a Christian Writer's Conference in Anchorage before Frank's surgery was scheduled.

"Frank, I don't know if I should leave you two weeks after a major surgery," I said.

"I feel good and I want you to go." His house robe hung loosely on his shoulders, and touches of gray streaked his hair. He had a determined look on his face and added, "You've stood by me when other women would have given up, and I want you to have this opportunity."

Tears flowed and laughter at the same time. I hugged him tight. "Thank you, I do so want to go. You're still feeling rough, but you're willing to take care of the girls. That means everything to me."

Sponsored by the local Bible College, the conference focused on writing for religious periodicals. Guest speakers included Sherwood Wirt a journalist and founder of *Decision Magazine* and Norman and Virginia Rohrer, authors from California. They critiqued one of my children's stories, *A Winning Choice*, and a Sunday school take-home paper paid me twenty-five dollars for it. If the amount had been one-hundred, I couldn't have been prouder.

The week flew by, and I returned to Glennallen to pack for the move back to the mobile home on Chena Hot Springs road in Fairbanks. Our previous landlord had suggested we stay there for the two weeks before we were to leave on our trip outside, and, when we returned, live there until Frank got another teaching position. We happily accepted his offer. The prospect of seeing our families after three years kept us from feeling too discouraged about the need to move again.

I wondered if we were crazy to take a vacation right then. We'd soon find out.

Chapter 19

On the Road Again

My grace is sufficient for you.
—*2 Corinthians 12:9*

Ruthie had been driving me crazy all afternoon. Every five minutes she asked, "When will they be here? Are they here yet?" Wide-eyed, my three-year-old jumping bean anticipated the arrival of her daddy and uncle Steve from the airport in Anchorage.

Steve was coming to help us move back to the mobile home on Chena Hot Springs Road in Fairbanks. While in Fairbanks, he would help Frank convert our travel trailer to a camping trailer. We planned to combine a trip to visit our families with travel to Pomona, California for Frank to take an education course. We would camp along the way—an activity we all enjoyed.

Steve planned to travel with us to Whitehorse, Yukon Territory, the first leg of our journey. At Whitehorse, he would leave us and join a friend in Skagway.

"Uncle Steve," Ruthie yelled, running down the front steps to meet him when he and Frank arrived.

"Great to see you," I said. "Thanks for coming to help us move."

"Glad to help. After all, Frank had major surgery three weeks ago and doesn't need to be lifting heavy furniture."

We traded hugs all around and went inside to get Steve settled for a good night's sleep after his long flight from Southern California.

For the next couple of days, we packed our household goods—furniture, kitchen ware, food and clothes—and loaded them into our travel trailer. The trailer measured seven feet wide, nine and one-half feet long, and six feet and one and one-half inches high. Our 1970 Volvo still had the trailer hitch on it.

*****

We arrived in Fairbanks after five hours of driving and unloaded everything into the mobile home. Frank and Steve immediately went to work, converting the trailer into a camper. They built two beds out of plywood with legs at two corners. The legs folded parallel to the end sides of each bed. The beds hinged to the interior sides of the trailer so they could be folded up each morning. Thick foam pads and a sleeping bag would make these comfortable. Because they doubled as a place to sit and eat, Frank allowed a narrow walk space between them.

For the girls' bunks, Frank first cut four heavy blocks of wood and nailed two of them to one side of the trailer, one toward the front and one toward the back. He did the same thing on the opposite wall of the trailer. The girls' bunks, made of two rectangular pieces of heavy sailcloth, would hang above ours like hammocks.

For both bunks, each side of the sailcloth was hemmed then folded over and sewn to form a pocket. Holes were drilled through each end of two one-inch dowel rods. One rod was slipped through a long pocket on one side of the bunk, and the other dowel rod slipped through the long pocket on the opposite side. The dowel closest to the wall of the trailer was laid atop the two wooden blocks nailed there and secured with two metal hooks. A thick rope was threaded through the end of the dowel and tied securely then threaded through the short pocket and through the dowel rod on the opposite long side. This was done on the other end of the bunk also.

The ends of the ropes of each bunk were looped and knotted to hang on four hooks attached to the ceiling.

"That's an ingenious idea, though I'm a little concerned that the girls might fall out," I said.

"We'll just have to make sure they don't bounce in their bunks," Frank replied.

"Right," I agreed because we had too much left to do to discuss it further.

Against the back wall, Frank built storage space and a shelf for the Coleman stove, with a small louvered window above it. He secured a hook screw on the ceiling to hang the Coleman lantern.

The men barely finished the conversion the day before we were to leave.

"The Volvo's tuned up and running well, but I wish we had time to do a trial run to test the camping trailer," Frank said, frowning.

"Me too. That's always a wise idea," Steve agreed.

"No can do, though. I need to be in Pomona for that education course the morning of July 8."

*****

Early on the morning of June 29, drive day, I looked out the window of the mobile home to see sleeping bags, a first-aid kit, the camp stove, an ice chest, two coils of rope, a tarpaulin, and boxes of groceries strewn around the trailer. *No way we will be on the road by noon,* I mumbled to myself. Frank and Steve proved me wrong.

They sorted, loaded, unloaded, and reloaded all the paraphernalia, while I hustled to pack clothes, toiletries, blankets, and pillows and kept track of Ruthie and Jeanne.

By noon, we were ready to go. "Time to load 'em up and move 'em out," Frank said.

We tried not to think about our limited space, limited time, and limited funds.

Our plans included a stop in Vancouver, British Columbia on July 4 to visit a former pastor, Gordon Phillips, and his wife, Eulalia. In San Francisco, we would visit friends before traveling on to Woodland Hills in Orange County and Frank's parents. We hoped to make it to his folks in time for Frank to get a good night's sleep before the fifty-mile drive to Pomona—clearly wishful thinking.

The Alaska Highway in 1980 was still gravel road for about 1,100 miles between Tok Junction, Alaska and Dawson Creek, British Columbia. Once again, we planned our daily drive with the help of our trusted friend, *The Milepost*. We had relied heavily on it during our journey north from California when we moved to Alaska. In the guide, distances in miles are listed from Delta Junction, the northern end of the Alaska Highway, or from Dawson Creek, the southern end.

*****

For the next several days, we became a rolling exhibition. People often asked about our two-toned-blue wooden camper that resembled a horse trailer. Frank explained how he had steamed and kerfed the plywood to get it to curve and how he designed the interior with fold up beds.

The trailer made driving tricky—like the tail wagging of the dog. Poor Frank had to do most of the driving because Steve had difficulty controlling the car and camper on the rough roads. And Frank refused to let me try it, for which I was grateful.

All afternoon, the rain poured down, with a brief interlude when we stopped that evening at a campground near Glennallen. We cooked on the Coleman stove and ate with the doors open to let the light shine in. Steve went to the outdoor privy after we ate before heading to his tent for the night. Immediately rain and hail pelted our trailer.

"I hope Steve doesn't get stuck in the john," Frank unwittingly commented.

Outdoor toilets terrified Ruthie, and she began howling. "Uncle Steve is stuck in the john. He's stuck in the john."

We tried to convince her that Frank had only meant Steve would have to stay in the outdoor toilet until the rain stopped to avoid getting wet. She didn't believe us. "Daddy, he fell in, go get him, go get him out," she repeated.

When the rain slowed, Frank put on his slicker and pretended to go see about "poor Uncle Steve."

"Uncle Steve's safe in his tent, Ruthie," Frank said when he returned.

He took off his wet slicker, picked her up, and hugged her tightly. "Now, let's try out our sleeping arrangements."

Frank and I lowered our beds and got the girls' bunks ready. Ruthie loved hers but had to have a pillow—she never wanted one unless there wasn't one. I gave her mine then sneaked it away after she fell asleep.

Jeanne was another story. She tossed and turned and began crying. I decided she might be cold because I had failed to bring enough blankets for the damp forty-degree weather. Jeanne came into my bunk with me. Later, Ruthie woke up.

"I'm cold," she said, crying.

Oh, brother. I put her next to me, let Jeanne sleep on my chest, and I covered us all with a blanket and a heavy parka which kept us warm, but did not help me sleep. It was a long night.

Frank and I woke early the next morning and managed to fix a cup of coffee on the Coleman stove before we woke the children. In an expansive mood, we lingered too long over coffee. By the time we fixed a hot breakfast, woke and fed the kids, broke camp, and bundled everyone into the car, two hours of our much-needed driving time were gone. Every morning after that, I woke the kids and dressed them, while Frank fixed coffee, and we all ate a quick bowl of cereal—the luxury of a hot meal could wait until evening.

At mid-morning of the second day, an alert driver passed us honking and gesturing toward the trailer.

"Wonder what's wrong," Steve said.

"We'd better find out," Frank said and pulled off the road. He and Steve sloshed through the rain to check the back of the trailer.

"What happened?" I asked when they returned.

"We forgot to remove the Coleman lantern from its hook, and when it fell, the mantle broke," Frank said with a sigh. "When we reach Whitehorse, I'll get another one."

"How did those people who passed us see the lantern fall?" I asked, puzzled.

Steve laughed. "The back door had jarred loose and swung open. We secured it with a heavy rope."

MOUNTAINS, RAINBOWS AND AN OCCASIONAL MOOSE

Rainy weather put us slightly behind schedule. We camped that night at Sourdough Creek, a Bureau of Land Management (BLM) campground on the Glenn Highway, near Tok. What a surprise to run into our friends Owen and Linda Fansler. Frank recognized their familiar yellow van, and we walked over and tapped on their door.

"Would you folks happen to be the Fanslers?" Frank asked.

"You think?" replied Owen. "Come on in before we're all soaked."

We crowded inside their camper and introduced Steve. Though we were elbow to elbow, with five adults and four children, no one seemed to mind.

"Remember our campout at Tangle Lake two years ago?" Frank asked.

"Yeah, it rained that weekend too," Owen replied.

"We still had fun," Linda and I agreed.

Laughing and talking with good friends is always the best way to spend time. After about an hour, we had to call it a night. We had a long day ahead of us. Owen and Linda loaned us a couple of extra blankets and told us to keep them till we returned. We all slept better, but Jeanne, still an infant, often vocalized her disapproval of the sleeping arrangements.

Beautiful sunny weather and seventy-degree temperatures blessed us Tuesday and helped us make better time. We were getting good gas mileage—seventeen miles per gallon—and the highest price so far was $1.52.

We drove by Kluane Lake, and its glacier-fed water shone like a turquoise jewel. The largest lake in the Yukon Territory, the Alaska Highway follows its southern border. We got out to stretch our legs at Boutillier Summit, elevation 3,293 feet, and the second highest point on the highway between Fairbanks and Whitehorse.

"Let's picnic here, on top of the world," I said, gazing at the spectacular view, wishing we had time to explore.

Like poet Robert Frost wrote, we had *miles to go* before we could sleep. One hundred miles of rugged mountain driving stretched between us and Whitehorse, Yukon Territory.

*****

We reached Whitehorse about four o'clock in the afternoon. On the way to the campground, we searched for a hardware store to buy a mantle for the broken lantern and other supplies and found most businesses closed.

"What's going on? Why is everything closed on a Tuesday?" Steve asked the campground manager.

"It's a holiday, Canada Day, July 1," the manager explained.

"Must be why this campground is so crowded too," Frank said.

"Yeah, we might as well be camping at Griffith Park in LA," Steve complained.

"Let's make the best of it. After all, today we had sunny weather, no mud," I said.

Besides, we were surrounded by upbeat Canadians, everyone friendly and in a holiday mood. That night in our bunks, we listened to the fireworks in the distance and wondered if we would make it to Vancouver, British Columbia by July 4.

*****

Steve left us for Skagway the next day to join his friend and hike the Chilkoot Trail. He had been most helpful with the move and the first leg of our journey. He was interested in geology and made an excellent guide, explaining rock formations along the way.

We headed to a campground about thirty miles from Watson Lake, Mile 777, the last town in Yukon Territory. The rest of our drive through Canada would be in British Columbia. The drive went well, but even after a restful night's sleep, we were unprepared for what turned out to be the most difficult day of the trip.

Leaving Watson Lake, Frank wanted to drive a route through Fort Nelson and Fort St. John and take the Hudson's Hope Loop, a shortcut around Dawson Creek. Driving gravel roads in an old car and wanting to enjoy scenery was not a combination for making good time. Neither had we paid enough attention to "Travel Tips for Toddlers," namely, they can't be hurried, don't like porta-potties, showers, or riding in their car seats and like to sleep during the day and run and play at night. By July 3, we knew we were in trouble.

Near Muncho Lake, the highway veered east, crossing crystal clear streams. Stone mountain sheep greeted us, joined by caribou that roamed the lake road. Lambs came right up to the car—traffic and people didn't frighten them.

"Can we pet them, Daddy?" Ruthie asked.

"They won't let us get that close," Frank explained. He pulled off the road and grabbed the movie camera. One mama goat approached us, looked fiercely at Frank, and tried to stick her head inside the car, to the delight of the girls. He shooed her away and shot a few more feet of film before we drove on.

Our newfound animal friends and the gorgeous scenery lulled us into a relaxed attitude toward our schedule. Reality bit not long after we passed Muncho Lake. We wanted to go—the car didn't.

The fuel pump caused vapor lock, and we could travel only a few miles between stops. Frank was forced to work under the car in the mud, mosquitoes, and heat, but he managed to remain calm, for the first few hours anyway. I admired his stamina. Ruthie and Jeanne thought the whole thing a new game; Daddy drove a few miles, the engine sputtered and stopped, Daddy got red in the face, and they were allowed to get out and run around, with me trying to corral them.

During one of the breakdowns, when Frank pulled off the road, I decided to look in the ice chest to see if we needed to pick up anything when we reached a town.

"Oh, no!" I yelled when I looked inside.

Yellow egg yolks and mustard had mixed with red ketchup and formed a gooey liquid in which the packages of bacon and bologna floated.

The egg keeper, guaranteed to prevent breakage, failed the test on the rough Alaska highway. Since griping never cleaned anything,

I attacked the chest, conquered it, and fixed us all a sandwich before we got back on the road.

Five hours and several delays later, Frank lost his cool, cursing the car and whatever else he could think of. I put my hands over my face and cried. He looked exhausted, and the kids were tired and hungry again. All the while, I prayed for someone to help us.

On a high mountain road, the car stopped again, and Frank pulled off onto a clearing. One side of the road was bordered by a towering cliff of sheer granite. The car was parked only four or five yards from a steep drop-off. Frank got out of the car and once again lifted the hood. A short while later, a car approached.

A man rolled his car window down and said, "You folks look like you might need some help." I saw a woman and three teenagers in the car.

"Thank God you stopped," Frank said in a shaky voice. "We've made only seventy miles in the last five hours. I think my car has vapor lock."

"Let's see," the man offered. Frank lifted the hood of the Volvo.

I thought to myself, *The man might be a top-notch mechanic, or just a friendly guy who knows nothing about cars, but we are desperate.*

The girls and I got out of our car and walked toward the other one. In its side mirror, I saw my tear-streaked face, unkempt hair; the kids with red Kool-Aid spilled down their fronts; and Frank covered in dirt and grease. A bunch of hippies.

"Seeing your car stop was an answer to prayer," I said to the man's wife. "We're on our way from Fairbanks to California to visit family."

"Tom's an air force motor pool mechanic. If he can't figure it out, no one can," she said.

She told me that her husband, a sergeant, was being transferred from Elmendorf Air Force Base in Anchorage to Florida, where they were headed.

The man returned to his car, lifted the trunk, and rummaged around until he found a box. Miracle of miracles, he had an electric fuel pump which fit our 1970 Volvo and he wanted to loan it to us. Of course, God knew about this all the time.

"Are you sure? I don't know what to say…" Frank's voice broke.

"Thank you," I added. I could hardly speak and trembled with relief.

The wiry sergeant, a man of few words, said, "You can buy a replacement and mail it back when you get where you're going. Now, let's get this thing installed."

Afterward, he and Frank exchanged addresses and shook hands. We waved to our benefactors as they drove away. Although the phrase "random acts of kindness" had not yet been coined, it certainly fit. Since that day, I have always remembered the sergeant as our guardian angel.

We covered the eighty miles to Fort Nelson with no more stops, rolled into town about eleven o'clock in the evening, and found a campground with vacancy and hot showers. What a welcome relief for our weary family.

Frank headed to bathe after we set up camp and put the sleeping girls in their bunks. Quiet sounds of night soothed me, and I once again thanked God for his watchful care over us. The kind sergeant traveling that isolated road with exactly what we needed was no coincidence—it was grace.

Chapter 20

A Winding Road

Make me to know your ways, O Lord; Teach me your paths.

—Psalm 25:4

We got back on the road about nine thirty the next morning after hot showers and a good night's sleep at the campground in Fort Nelson, British Columbia. The stop-and-go nightmare of the previous day earned us a sleep-in. Prayers were offered that the new fuel pump would keep our old Volvo going.

Sure enough, the morning rolled by smoothly. We stopped for lunch at Charlie Lake, a small community named for the body of water it bordered. We picnicked in a park surrounded by white birch trees full of song birds, next to a playground constructed of logs with swings and slides—a delightful find for the children. They loved it, and so did Frank and I. He took my hand.

"Why don't we stop and live here away from the rest of the world?" he whispered. I smiled but said nothing, not wanting to clutter the moment with words.

Sitting in that tranquil place, I understood why early pioneers often settled in a pleasant valley instead of traveling further West.

We sat there for several moments before Frank's voice cut into my thoughts.

"Come on, girls, it's time to go."

At this, Ruthie stomped her foot and said, "No go." Her dad picked her up, I gathered Jeanne, and we headed to the car with two howling children. Frank bribed them with gumballs from the service station dispenser. This turned out to be a rather messy solution because the pink candy got all over their faces and hands and dripped down their shirt fronts on to the upholstery. A quick wash off later and the warm sun soon lulled them to sleep.

Frank and I revived ourselves with coffee from the thermos. We enjoyed driving through the Peace River Valley—which is exactly that—peaceful with lush farmland, clear rivers, and streams. Trains hummed along through mountain tunnels. British Columbia with its mountains, meadows, and verdant landscape is one of Canada's jewels.

By Friday, July 4, we had accepted that our stop in Vancouver was not going to happen. We reached the end of the 1,100 miles of gravel road at four o'clock that afternoon. Once again, we had conquered the worst part of the Alaska Highway—something to celebrate.

In Fort St. John, we found Windmar Campground, owned by Howard Wilson and his wife, an older couple, friendly, helpful, and still enjoying life. We parked the car and trailer next to a picnic table, and I set the girls free while I prepared a hasty supper.

A white cat interrupted our meal. The girls lost interest in eating to pet the kitty who indulged them for a few minutes then made a hasty retreat.

I took them with me after supper to Mrs. Wilson's ceramic shop in one corner of the campground office. Her husband was enamored by toddler charm and showed them six soft furry kittens. He also had a couple of horses. With such entertainment, I had a hard time convincing the girls it was time to bathe and go to bed.

"Here, use our bathtub," Mrs. Wilson said when she saw me try to get the girls into the shower.

"How kind…but, we don't want to impose," I protested, to no avail. Ruthie brightened at the idea of a bath instead of a shower, and my attitude toward bath time improved, because bathing a three-year-old and an infant of eighteen months in a shower is like bathing frogs in a pond.

I awoke the next morning with a sore throat. Ruthie, Jeanne, and I headed to the office—me, for throat lozenges and them, to see the kittens.

"Here they are, girls." Mr. Wilson pointed to the box of wriggly fur.

"Please join me for a cup of coffee, eh?" He indicated a chair and poured me a cup, before I could answer.

"Have you and Mrs. Wilson always lived in British Columbia?" I asked.

"Oh, no, we moved west about thirty years ago when Calgary got too crowded."

"How long have you owned the campground?"

"Since 1970. Before that, I was in real estate, and we managed restaurants. A campground is a good fit for our retirement years because we enjoy camping and meeting a variety of people. Now British Columbia is more crowded than we like, but that's progress, eh?"

"Crowded." I chuckled. "We're headed to Los Angeles. Now that's crowded."

When Frank drove up, we coaxed Ruthie and Jeanne away from the kittens. Impulsively, I hugged Mr. and Mrs. Wilson. "Thank you so much for your kindness. People like you have made our long journey a lot shorter."

*****

Our day proved uneventful, but Jeanne gave us quite a scare at bedtime, when she bounced in her bunk and fell out. Her "guardian angel" rescued her from near injury when she came within an inch of the Coleman lantern. She landed on our bedrolls, so no broken bones.

I awoke Sunday morning unable to speak except in a hoarse voice and felt achey all day. We crossed the border and stopped for gas near Seattle. Mount St. Helens had erupted in May, and Steve, who was a geology student, had asked us to collect a sample of volcanic dust. We found plenty in patches of dirt along the highway.

By nightfall, we reached Southern Oregon, not far from the California state line. The drive to Woodland Hills where Frank's mother lived would take us fifteen to seventeen hours, and the education workshop scheduled for Tuesday morning was about fifty miles from Woodland Hills.

We stopped in the San Francisco Bay area Monday afternoon for a quick supper with college friends, Clyde and Alice Horn. By this time, my voice was completely gone.

"Sure wish we could stay for a visit like we planned. We've got to push on though," Frank said. He looked glum, and with tears in my eyes, I hugged Alice. We hadn't seen them since we'd left California in '75.

"Don't worry about it. The same thing has happened to us. We understand," Clyde told Frank.

"Traveling's that way," Alice added. "Clyta, write me a letter when you get back home."

With that, we were on our way again. The smooth surface of California roads far surpassed the gravel of the Alaska Highway. No argument there. Still, Frank had to pull a camping trailer in traffic and compete with truckers. The route had steep inclines and curves to negotiate. I was surprised when he said, "Why don't you take the wheel for a while, Clyta. Just go slow and hold her steady."

"Well, okay, I'll try. There's less traffic here on the Central Coast."

He must be desperate, I thought.

After a couple of hairpin curves between San Luis Obispo and Santa Barbara, with the trailer weaving back and forth, my husband became fully alert again and told me to pull over!

We rolled into Woodland Hills about one o'clock in the morning. Mom Dennin had beds ready, and the girls never woke up. Poor Frank had to leave by seven thirty the next morning in order to get to Pomona by nine o'clock.

Later he said he didn't remember a whole lot about the Assertive Discipline course except that it took a lot of discipline for him to stay awake. He collapsed into bed soon after he returned from Pomona that evening.

*****

"Steve, how did the hike over the Chilkhoot trail go?" Frank asked the next morning.

"The scenery and rock formations were beautiful." Steve laughed. "The trail was so steep that I spent most of the time sliding down it on my butt. I developed an admiration for the gold seekers of 1898."

We all laughed at that!

*****

Ruthie turned four while we were in the lower forty-eight. Tom, Frank's stepfather, and Steve also had July birthdays, so the next two weeks became a collage of parties, gifts, and a trip to Disneyland, which in 1980 cost around twenty-five dollars a head. My sore throat had healed, and I enjoyed the activities.

Ruthie fell in love with Mickey Mouse, and "It's A Small World After All" entranced her. All the Mickeys running around with big ears scared Jeanne, and when poor Goofy patted her on the head, she screamed.

*****

When it was time to head to Arkansas and Oklahoma, I think the old car actually groaned; however, there was nothing to do but roll on. Frank had found a good deal on an air conditioner for the car and had it installed so we could drive in cool comfort. That was the plan anyway. We did make it across the Mojave Desert before the Volvo's unreliable electrical system and the new air conditioner became incompatible.

No rain or mud, just unbearable heat accompanied us. A stop at the home of Bill and Brenda Lee in West Texas and at another friend's home in El Dorado, Oklahoma offered brief respites from ninety-degree temperatures. We thanked both families, but I doubt that either understood how much their hospitality meant to us. The words of an old gospel hymn say it well:

A home within the wilderness, A rest upon the way. From the burning of the noontide heat and the burden of the day.

*****

We stopped first in Fort Smith to spend a week with Frank's dad, his stepmother, Elsie, sister, Judy, and his grandmother. Because of their small house, we shared a room with Ruthie and Jeanne. Mr. Coder, a loud and boisterous man, loved to tease his mother's chihuahua, which caused the little dog to bark ferociously and Grandma Coder to protest.

After a week, we left the camping trailer there and drove to Tulsa where my family lived. Grandmother had come over to Mother's apartment to greet us when we arrived.

"Come in out of the heat," Mother said. She embraced me and then Frank.

Grandmother embraced us next, and we all laughed and cried at the same time.

The grandmothers chose to let the girls come to them in their own time, and it wasn't long before Ruthie and Jeanne were sitting on their laps and listening while they read stories to them. Now that I have grandchildren of my own, I realize how hard it must have been for our families to see us for only a brief time, with months and sometimes years in between.

Grandparents and children had a wonderful time, and Frank and I enjoyed being with parents, sisters, and brothers-in-law too. Mother and Grandmother and each of my sisters and their families went out of their way to make us feel comfortable. One Sunday Linda and her husband, Don, were dealing with air conditioning problems and still hosted Sunday dinner for everyone. Another sister, Billie, invited the girls and me to spend one Friday night with her.

Carolyn flew from Houston to join us—a joyful reunion, especially for me because I had not seen her since 1973.

My grandmother and I had always been very close, and it was difficult for her to accept my living so far away. She somehow made room for us to stay a few days with her in the tiny retirement apartment where she lived. Cooking was Grandmother's way to show love, so we ate three big meals a day with desserts like chocolate fudge pie, Italian cream cake, and Frank's favorite, raisin pie. Everyone expected us to eat heartily, and we obliged.

*****

With no job awaiting his return, Frank and I struggled to be cheerful. My mother was the only one we told our true situation—we had to talk to someone about it.

A couple of days before we left, when she and I were alone, Mother looked at me, her brown eyes filled with concern. "Clyta, you and the girls are welcome to stay with me until you know whether Frank has a job," she said.

"Thanks, Mom," I squeezed her hand. "But if Frank gets a teaching position, he won't have time to come back for us, and we can't afford to fly."

"I understand. The last few years must have been pretty hard for him."

"Yes, he's hurting, and I feel my place is with him." I paused for a moment and said, "We're not ready to give up on Alaska."

"But, where will you live?"

"Mr. Herning has already said we could stay in the mobile home on his property as long as we need to. We will make it, we always have."

"I admire your faith and determination."

"Mom, *you* gave it to me. You struggled to raise us and showed by example what it means to love sacrificially."

In the months ahead, we would need a lot of that faith and determination.

Chapter 21

Kansas City and Beyond

> *Now faith is the substance of things hoped for, the evidence of things not seen.*
> —*Hebrews 11:1 (KJV)*

After staying a week in Tulsa, Frank had gone back to Fort Smith, Arkansas to spend time with his father, tune up the car, and make any needed repairs to the trailer, while the girls and I remained there for another week. On Sunday, my mother and sisters Millie and Linda drove us to Fort Smith to join him. We laughed and talked and enjoyed being together to overcome the undercurrent of sadness as we faced another goodbye. I had not told Millie and Linda of Frank's teaching difficulties in Cordova and Glennallen, and I knew by the puzzled looks on their faces that they suspected something was wrong, though they didn't press me.

One of the things I remember most about the 1980 vacation was the heat. We weren't used to one-hundred-degree temperatures. The girls' faces were always flushed and their hair damp with sweat—the day we left was no exception. Since Frank had given up on the car's air conditioner, we faced several hours of uncomfortable heat. After long hugs and many kisses and tears, we bid our families goodbye and headed north.

*****

I flunked map reading in Kansas City—got us off on a drag through the city instead of the freeway around it. We saw what we thought was a service station and pulled in to check the map. It turned out to be a police substation and, to make things more interesting, when Frank turned the car around, he clipped a large trailer belonging to the police department.

Frank groaned. "I didn't see that thing," he said, getting out to inspect the damage.

A police sergeant approached—a man of about fifty. He was sympathetic to our story, and since no harm had come to the trailer, he told us we could go on. Before we had a chance to leave, a young whipper-snapper officer arrived and insisted on making a complete inquiry. Frank clenched his jaws and followed the young man inside, while the girls and I sat in the hot car. The older officer apologized, brought us some water, and jotted down names and directions to a few budget motels on the northwest side of the city.

About fifteen minutes later, after a thorough investigation, the officer-in-charge fined us forty dollars and let us go.

Frank threw an angry look over his shoulder, cursed under his breath, and glared at me. "Clyta, will you ever learn to read a map?"

"Probably not," I replied. In a calm voice, I said, "It's too hot to camp tonight. We can afford one motel. The sergeant gave me directions and said there's a McDonald's on the way."

"Thanks. Sorry I yelled and criticized your…uh…map reading." We began to laugh—we were exhausted and slaphappy—the laughter released tension.

Since then, Kansas City has never been one of my favorite places, but I'll always love Saint Jo. For on the other side of Saint Joseph, Missouri the next day, the temperature dropped about twenty degrees. A fresh wind blew our gloom away.

*****

We journeyed north through Nebraska and the Dakotas, bid the USA farewell and crossed into Saskatchewan to traverse Canada on Highway One. With no traffic and flat roads, I was able to relieve

Frank now and then. The drive became a patchwork of corn and wheat fields, broken by a grain silo every fifty miles or so—the bread basket of Canada.

One of the differences in driving cross-country in the 1980s was that we couldn't text or call on a cell phone to let our families know how things were going. Neither could Frank easily contact a school district by phone. In Red Deer, a fairly large Saskatchewan town, he used a pay phone to call Fairbanks North Star Borough. It took him a while to get through, but it didn't matter because the district had no teaching positions to offer him anyway. His shoulders slumped, and he looked grim as he walked back to the car.

*****

We continued our trek across the prairie, stopping the next Saturday at a combination gas station-country store. After we filled the tank and used the restroom, the manager invited us to join him in front of the television where we rested a while and laughed at the antics of Abbott and Costello.

On Sunday, we attended worship in a small community church in Alberta. A smiling woman approached us. "Good morning. I'm Margie, and we're so glad to have you today."

We introduced ourselves and explained that we were on our way back from Oklahoma and Arkansas to Fairbanks, Alaska.

"A long way," she said. "Please join us after church for a potluck dinner. There will be plenty of food—enough to feed a small army I'd say."

We accepted her invitation. The congregation was friendly and welcoming.

While driving, we talked about what might happen when we reached Fairbanks. Would Frank get another teaching position? What if he didn't? Should we take our chances or collect our furniture and goods, pack up, and head back to Oklahoma? We loved Alaska, had made a lot of friends, and didn't want to leave, but we had two children and needed to make a living.

One evening, after a day of rain, the sun came out. We pulled into a campground, and after supper, took a walk to stretch our legs. Frank held Ruthie's hand, and Jeanne and I toddled slowly behind.

"Look, Daddy, a rainbow, God's promise," Ruthie said and pointed to the sky. She had heard the story of Noah and the ark and how God had placed a rainbow in the sky—a sign of his promise never to flood the earth again.

"Yes, honey, God's promise," Frank answered.

Back in our trailer, we tossed and turned after we got the kids to sleep that night.

"You still awake, Clyta?"

"Yes."

"I wish that rainbow had been a neon sign telling me what to do. I'm so confused," Frank said.

"Well, I know one thing. Whatever happens, whether we stay in Alaska only a few more months or for several years, God's promise is that he will be with us."

Chapter 22

One Day at a Time

I will counsel you and teach you the way you should go: I will counsel you with my eye upon you.
—*Psalm 32:8*

Back in Fairbanks

In the following year and a half, the rainbow promise strengthened us through challenges and change. Thanks to Carl and Mattie Lee Herning, we had a roof over our heads when we returned to Fairbanks. Carl did not want to accept rent for the mobile home on his property because that would alter his tax status. However, food, gas, clothes, and other necessities did require income. We had decided I would not go back to work unless it was absolutely necessary because our two young children, one eighteen months and the other four years, needed my care.

Frank interviewed for a teaching position in Kodiak. Kodiak is the largest island of a cluster of small islands and is located in the Gulf of Alaska, southwest of the Kenai Peninsula. After he talked to several people who had lived in Kodiak, we decided the isolation would be intolerable for us.

He applied for every teaching position he heard about, but he received no offers. During the fall and winter months, he looked for other types of work and collected unemployment.

"I feel such a failure," he often said. My heart ached for him. A letter I wrote to Mother described my yearning to help him.

> I recently read "Saul" a poem by Robert Browning based on the story of King Saul and the shepherd David. The poem is written from David's perspective and expresses my feelings about Frank.
>
> Do I find love so full in my nature,
> God's ultimate gift,
> That I doubt His own love can compete with it?
> here, the parts shift
> Here, the creature surpass the Creator,
> the end, what Began?
> Would I fain in my impotent yearning
> do all for this man,
> And dare doubt He alone shall not help
> him, who yet alone can?

For my part, I prayed for him and stood by him. Before we left Fairbanks for Cordova in 1979, we had attended Moose Creek Baptist Church where Frank directed the choir in a Christmas cantata. We joined the church again in September, and Frank joined the choir and sometimes directed when Stan, the regular director, could not be there. Pastor Ed Conners,* his wife, Virginia, and our friends in the church provided a support system. (*The names of the pastor and his family have been changed.)

Psalm 119:105 tells us that God's word is a lamp to our feet and a light to our path. The Baptist Convention in 1980 printed a guideline for reading the entire Bible in a year. Reading scripture each day helped me take God's word into my heart and focus my mind on God's love and His plan for our lives, rather than on the problems we faced. At the same time, I learned of a program of Bible memorization for children and adults. Ruthie memorized simple verses like "God is love" (1 John 4:8), and I began memorizing the first book of John.

Each week we met with a friend and repeated the verses we had learned. (I hope no one who reads this expects me to quote verbatim the entire first book of John; after all, that was over thirty years ago.) For me, the important concept was to allow God's Word to become a part of me and guide my thinking.

The adult Sunday school class Frank taught encouraged him to study the Bible also. I have found it to be true that our faith is strengthened more during times of struggle and hurt than in times when life goes smoothly.

Friends Owen and Linda Fansler listened to our concerns without criticism or judgment—we had the assurance that conversations with them would not be repeated. We shared meals, outings, and holidays with them and their two children Darcie and Kevin, who were about the same age as our girls. When burdens are shared, they become lighter.

*****

In addition to time spent with friends and Bible study, opportunities to serve others also came my way. Once again, I had the opportunity to work with my friend Valeria Sherard at Friendship Mission. She called me one evening.

"Clyta, how are you? I heard you and Frank were back in town."

"Yes. The teaching situation in Glennallen didn't go as we'd hoped," I said, and added, "I've been thinking about calling you."

"Would you be interested in helping us on Monday night? I have a group of girls, aged eight to ten, who need a teacher," Valeria said."

"You know I would. Frank can bring me when he goes to the community chorus at the university, but Ruthie and Jeanne will need to come with me. Is that all right?"

"Sure. The girls can be in the preschool class."

"Good, that will give them a chance to be with other children."

Valeria's half of this conversation took a while because she hailed from Mississippi and never got in a hurry.

The next Monday evening, I took Ruthie and Jeanne with me to Friendship Mission to teach stories and songs to a group of girls, aged eight to ten. They were lively students and curious about the cultures of other countries. Planning crafts and activities for them was fun. Interaction with the children provided writing ideas also.

The writers' conference I attended before we left Glennallen had inspired me to keep writing, though with two active children, that was not easy. However, I persevered and writing became a creative outlet and a healing therapy for me, like music comforted Frank.

*****

Our entertainments were simple. Carl and Mattie Lee loaned us a television, and we already had a radio. They had a satellite dish, which enabled us to get at least one of the commercial stations, but our favorites were Public Television and National Public Radio which provided a window to the world.

Mattie Lee introduced us to a new program on PBS, *All Creatures Great and Small,* based on the books by James Herriot about a veterinarian in Yorkshire, England. We quickly became fans of both the books and the television series.

NPR carried *Adventures in Good Music* hosted by Karl Haas, and another classical music program, *Osborg's Choice,* broadcast from the Bay of Fundy in Nova Scotia. Father Osborg had a deep basso profundo voice which I will never forget. In fact, Ruthie and Jeanne enjoyed imitating him. Both programs featured classical music. Frank loved the music of Johann Sebastian Bach. Therefore, my kids, from the time they were born, heard the music of the great composer.

Nineteen-eighty began our long love affair with *A Prairie Home Companion,* hosted by Garrison Keilor, and the unforgettable citizens of "'Lake Woebegone, the little town that time forgot." Every Saturday night for the next fifteen years found the Coder family tuned in to hear a variety of good music and the latest news from Lake Woebegon. Because of NPR, I probably have the only children who were raised on a combination of Bach and *Prairie Home Companion.*

Exercise and time with our children joined hands to ease the strain of unemployment and helped us avoid cabin fever. The hillside meadow behind our trailer was packed with snow by late November. We ordered a sled and took the girls sledding as often as possible.

It might be dark at three o'clock in the afternoon, but the moon shining on the meadow lit our way as Frank and I took turns cross-country skiing. White snow sparkled under the stars and contrasted with the darkness of the bare limbed bushes bordering the meadow and our mobile home.

Before we knew it, the holidays were upon us. In December, the *Fairbanks Daily News-Miner* published my inspirational article, "The Light of Life."

> Into a dark world the Light was born. God's chosen people looked for a King to come in glory. God's chosen glory is not always the glory of our choosing... The Light came to earth in a simple way—a simple birth to humble parents, in a manger, in an obscure village. Each December the world pauses to celebrate God's gift of light, His Son.
>
> The lights of the Christmas season lend warmth to our celebration. Candles...tiny blinking lights of red, blue and green decorate our tree and homes. Yet as we consider Christ as the Light of the world and search for a light worthy to represent Him, we look for something more spectacular. The Northern sky gives the answer.
>
> Who has seen an aurora borealis without being filled with light? A flaming aurora throws splashes of green, red, and sometimes violet across a black sky in a miracle of light... The night of Christ's birth, the "the glory of the Lord" shining round about the shepherds, must have lit up the sky as brilliantly as an aurora. Shepherds and scholars watched, listened and beheld a miracle.

Their world was filled with light when the Light was born that night.

The darkness of the world longs for...an aurora of love, filling the dark night of men's souls, rekindling the flickering spark of hope within—changing a dark future into a prism of promise.

Changes

Frank continued to sing and help direct the choir at church throughout the winter. In May, 1981, the church voted to call him as minister of music. At the time, it seemed like an answer to prayer. Frank's unemployment compensation had ended and we did not want to take undue advantage of Mr. Herning's kindness. He had been generous to us, but it was time to move on.

"You know, I feel kind of uneasy about the position," Frank told me one evening after supper. "Ed wants the church to pay me a larger salary than he will be getting since he has a good retirement from the air force."

"That doesn't make sense to me either. Better discuss it more thoroughly with him and the deacons."

When Frank met with the pastor and deacons, he learned the real reason: the pastor needed time to build a house on land he had purchased. Frank would be carrying most of the load until Ed finished the house. Pastor Conners assured him that he would still be preaching at the two Sunday services and would be available to discuss any problems that came up during the week.

"What I really need is to work as a team with a stable pastor who has a strong relationship with a congregation," Frank told me after the meeting.

We talked about the pros and cons and prayed about the offer, and Frank decided to step out on faith and accept the position.

In June, we moved to an apartment not far from the church and that made it easier for Frank to do his job and for our family to be more involved in church activities. We made the best of apartment living—not our favorite lifestyle—especially when the apartment right over us was occupied by a family of four rambunctious boys.

I have heard it said that you usually don't get to know your neighbors in an apartment complex. That didn't apply in this case. During our time there, I became acquainted with several people and was able to reach out to some who were lonely and invite them to the church.

Summertime meant retreats, conferences, activities for youth and children, and Vacation Bible School. There were also opportunities to minister to new military families.

Escape Artists

We kept happily busy that summer even though it rained a lot in June and every day in July. Inclement weather was simply a part of living in Alaska, and we worked around it. Rainy summers are probably hardest on young people and children. They are free from school and want to get outdoors. Therefore, it was unfortunate for our church youth, and for me, that the first sunny day was also the first day of Vacation Bible School, which their parents insisted they attend. They did not want to be there.

The person who had been asked to help me teach the middle school youth had been sent on temporary duty (TDY) at the last minute. I had taught youth that age for a number of years and was well prepared. We met in a small room and though most years I had a more balanced mix of girls and boys, this year I was blessed with twelve boys aged twelve to fourteen and one girl. Let me repeat, they were *not* thrilled to be there.

Two boys climbed out the window the first day. Since I could hardly climb out the window to retrieve them, I soldiered on and taught my lesson plan to the remaining kids, who behaved pretty well.

One of the deacons had seen the boys exit the window and told their mother of their misbehavior. She called me that evening.

"If you have any more trouble with them or their brother, you let me know."

The boys were exemplary the rest of the week and for parents' night helped put together a funny quiz show incorporating the week's Bible stories.

By the end of VBS, I was exhausted and thankful that we had planned a camping trip near Salcha. We had everything packed and ready to go in order to leave Sunday evening after the parents' night program. August still allowed daylight until ten or eleven at night. Our three-day respite offered sunshine and mild temperatures, a combination of quiet time and recreational activities such as canoeing and wading in the cold water. We put our worries aside, relaxed, and enjoyed our girls.

Wednesday afternoon and time to return to reality came too soon.

*****

Weeks of rain caused delays on the building of the pastor's house. Several times the pastor was unavailable when problems came up that Frank needed to discuss with him. His absence hurt the church and put a strain on relationships within his family.

*****

In September, Ruthie started to kindergarten at the elementary school on Eilson Air Force Base. She rode the bus to school, and we picked her up each day at noon. Another couple in the apartments had a daughter in her class and suggested carpooling—a welcome suggestion since Frank and I had to share the car.

School was a difficult adjustment for my shy little girl, and I suffered the usual angst of a mother whose first child is off to school. Wasn't it only yesterday that she was born?

The first day, I asked her, "Well, Ruthie, did you like school?"

"Yes. I'm hungry," she replied, eyeing the peanut butter sandwiches on the table. "Dawn says we don't have to go back tomorrow."

"What?"

"School's only one day," Ruthie said and took a bite of her sandwich.

"No, honey, school will be Monday through Friday every morning until holidays and summer vacation. After a few days, you and Dawn will like it better." And they did. Frank and I and Dawn's parents had to laugh at their misunderstanding.

Jeanne was talking a lot more by then. She kept close to my side, "helping" me with the house cleaning and laundry. I'll never forget her first prayer. I had somehow got the car stuck in a snow bank on a road close to the apartment. We walked back home, and I called Frank, who wasn't too happy with me.

"Let's pray about it, Jeanne," I said and took her tiny hand in mine. She prayed, "Mommy. Daddy. Car. Help." The simplicity of that prayer has always remained with me.

Uncrafts

With one child at school, I had more time for other things. That fall, the Women's Missionary Union asked me to help them make stuffed animals to give to a children's home. They handed me a pattern for a frog and gave me hurried verbal instructions, which I should have written down. But, no, it looked so easy.

And it would have been easy had I noticed that the pattern was for one half of the frog and needed to be placed on the fold to be cut. The first one looked a little peculiar. Because I didn't have much time to devote to the project and wanted to get them finished as soon as possible, I ignored the peculiar shape and continued cutting, sewing, and stuffing. I completed six frogs to give to the WMU president at the next meeting.

Betty's face upon receiving the frogs was a puzzle. To her credit, she didn't laugh.

"Clyta, let's take these in the dining room and you can join us for a cup of coffee."

One of the stuffed frogs, sewn undoubtedly by a woman who knew what she was doing, was on the table, surrounded by several of the seated women. I sat down, picked it up, and noted that it looked nothing like mine. It looked like a frog.

My sense of humor rescued me, and my laughter gave Betty the freedom to laugh too. I reached in and pulled out one of my "half frogs" to show everyone, and soon we were all laughing hysterically.

Punctuated phrases erupted from me, "So embarrassed…can't believe I did that."

"At least you tried," Betty said. "We have thirty animals made so we only need ten more, anyway. No harm done."

Except to my pride.

Our Cabin Thanksgiving

The autumn days grew shorter, snow fell, and still on many days the pastor was away from the church trying to finish his house. By November, we needed a break to gain some objectivity.

"Let's rent the Fred Blixt cabin from the Bureau of Land Management for the Thanksgiving holiday," Frank suggested.

"A good idea," I agreed.

The rustic cabin, located in the White Mountains about sixty miles from Fairbanks on the Elliott Highway, had been built in 1935 by a Swedish trapper.

We had once spent a few days there and knew to take our Coleman stove, fuel, water, firewood, food, and bedding. With turkey and the trimmings and two kids in the back seat, we drove up early Thanksgiving morning. Tension eased with each mile.

Frank got a fire going in the old woodstove, and soon the cabin was cozy. The girls ran and tumbled on the creaking wooden floor.

"Book, Mommy, read," Jeanne toddled over with a bedraggled grey ledger.

"Let's see what it says," I said, opening it. "Jeanne, this is a guest book, look." I pointed to the signatures of visitors and their home towns and read a few to her. Among the signatures were people from Maine to Los Angeles and a few foreign countries.

She lost interest quickly. Ruthie had found something more interesting—an old Monopoly game.

Ruthie who was five years-old, kind of got the hang of the game but thought she should keep some of the money. Jeanne, almost three, stuffed the miniature houses, hotels, and game pieces into the pockets of her jeans. Every time I pulled them out, her chubby fingers sneaked them back in. A rather hilarious evening led to a long night.

Frank and I climbed the rustic ladder to sleep in the loft and bedded the girls downstairs.

"We forgot the main drawback to this loft arrangement," Frank complained, around midnight.

"I know. Heat rises. The girls are comfy on the ground floor, while we roast up here."

We endured sauna conditions in the loft, though it was minus twenty degrees outside. The cabin was not too far from the Dalton Road, or the haul road, which led North to the Prudhoe Bay Oil fields. Our night was punctuated with the occasional roar of an eighteen-wheeler.

When we arrived back in Fairbanks, I found several plastic houses, hotels, and a tiny metal hat in the pockets of Jeanne's pants. They remained among my keepsakes for a long, long time.

Chapter 23

Facing Future

> *For surely I know the plans I have for you, says the Lord, plans for your welfare and not for harm, to give you a future with hope.*
> —Jeremiah 29:11

Several choir members that Christmas of 1981 wanted to sing a cantata such as John W. Peterson's *Night of Miracles*, others agreed with Frank and asked, "Why don't we sing something different this year?"

He chose to have the choir sing *In the Bleak Midwinter*, Gustave Holst's beautiful setting of Christina Rosetti's poem. The text contrasts the lowly birth of the Son of God in a stable in the middle of winter with the desire of the poet to give him a worthy gift—her heart.

> *In the bleak midwinter frosty wind made moan.*
> *Earth stood hard as iron, water like a stone.*
> *Snow had fallen, snow on snow, snow on snow.*
> *In the bleak midwinter long ago...*
> *What can I give him, poor as I am?*
> *If I were a shepherd I would bring a lamb;*
> *If I were a wise man I would do my part.*
> *Yet what can I give him?*
> *Give my heart.*

Temperatures of minus thirty degrees in December didn't inspire people to come to choir practice. In spite of this, on Christmas Eve, our small choir performed a service of Christmas music that included Holst's piece, an arrangement of *Oh, Holy Night*, and congregational singing of Christmas carols.

"Frank, the music was beautiful. I love that Rosetti poem," one church member said.

"Yes. And the singing of 'Peace, Peace' with 'Silent Night' during the candle lighting was a perfect end to the service," her husband added.

We went home with a full heart.

Our friends Owen and Linda were out of town, so we spent Christmas day with a church member and her children. She had separated from her husband and was having a tough time. We laughed and talked and ate lots of baked ham and ambrosia. For dessert, we ate the fudge my grandmother had sent and drank spiced tea and coffee.

Soon the holiday season pushed 1981 out the door and 1982 rolled in.

*****

One evening after Christmas, Frank came home looking tired and drawn. I went to him and put my arms around him.

"We had a brief staff and deacon's meeting this afternoon. The deacons feel it's time for Ed to resume his full pastoral duties and don't think the church can pay a full-time salary and a minister of music too."

"What did Ed say?"

Frank frowned. "Problems at home have worsened and he doesn't know how much longer he can remain as pastor."

I stood up and paced the floor. "This is so unfair. They've made you the scapegoat for the pastor's lack of leadership while he built a house instead of a church."

"We could have had a successful ministry here," Frank lamented.

My thoughts jumbled together. *If only Frank had received the guidance he needed—however, "if only" is rubbish.*

"You were doing a good job. This isn't your fault. The congregation knew when they hired you that the pastor would resume full duties when he finished the house."

"Yes. I am caught in the middle."

The words of Christina Rosetti in the anthem setting we sang at Christmas characterized our mixed emotions. We knew our life in Alaska might be drawing to a close, and because we loved living there, our hearts sank like a stone. Our future looked bleak.

To give ourselves time to think, I returned to my sewing and Frank put on a recording of Bach for healing and consolation.

Later that night, after the children were in bed, I turned to Jeremiah 29:11 and read. "For surely I know the plans I have for you," says the Lord, "plans for your welfare and not for harm, to give you a future with hope."

The words brought peace and I thanked God for his promise.

*****

Some of our deepest friendships were formed in Alaska, and friendship is a forever blessing that lifts the spirit. On Saturday afternoon, friends from the church, Jim and Judy Cabe, made an unexpected visit.

"We brought hamburgers and all the fixin's for ice cream sundaes," Judy said.

"What a nice surprise," I greeted them.

"I never turn down ice cream," Frank said.

"Ice cream. Ice cream," the girls shouted, jumping up and down.

I cleared the table of boxes, and we gathered around it. Soon we munched on juicy barbequed hamburgers. Afterward, we had chocolate and strawberry sundaes. Yummy!

Jeanne succeeded in getting as much chocolate syrup down her front as in her mouth.

Judy's daughter and son took Ruthie and Jeanne to their room and read to them while the adults drank spiced tea and talked.

"We want you to know we love you and are praying for you," Judy said.

"We would love to see you stay at the church, but will certainly understand your decision," Jim added.

Their visit and the voiced concern of many others gave us hope, though the church didn't feel they could keep Frank on salary, and he resigned at the next business meeting.

*****

A couple of days after his resignation, Frank came home with a letter from Bein and Fushi in Chicago. The company made stringed instruments, a process known as luthiery. Several weeks earlier, Frank had shown me their recruitment ad in a woodworking magazine. He had casually mentioned that it sounded like an interesting possibility. I had dismissed it as a pipe dream.

"Chicago! You want us to move to Chicago?" Disbelief caused me to stare open-mouthed and speak more sharply than intended.

"Not us, just me. You and the girls could stay in Tulsa with your family until I begin earning money."

"And live on what?" I asked angrily.

"You'll have to get a part-time job and I'll borrow money on the insurance policy."

A heated argument ended with me crying, Frank cursing, and nothing solved. No better idea came to mind, and Frank looked determined, so I accepted his decision.

Frank and I, if nothing else, had developed a sense of humor in the face of challenges. For comic relief, during the days ahead, we referred to the violin makers as Fine and Bushy. Laughing at the situation reduced the uncertainty, made it less frightening.

The pastor's attitude was a mixture of sympathy and guilt. Frank spent most of his time in Ed's heated garage rebuilding the engine of the 1974 Mercury Comet he had bought. He had sold the Volvo and hoped to sell the '71 Maverick.

In those dark days, our lives turned to slush like spring breakup. We longed for solid footing; instead, our Alaskan winter melted and threatened never to be the same again. We knew we must leave Alaska. However, while Ruthie was at school and Jeanne was with a friend, I stole moments to meditate and seek God's peace.

Packing books one day, I came across a quotation from a Ringling Brothers Circus announcer: "Don't cry because it's over, smile because it happened." Alaska had given us much to smile about. We had two beautiful daughters. Friends like Mabel Cary had inspired us with their courage. Mabel had lost her husband in her fifties with two children to raise. Instead of giving up, she served the Lord bravely for many years after. Mabel inspired me to serve joyfully, even when things were not going my way. I remembered her courage in 1999 when I lost my husband to cancer and walked the same path.

*****

Like our peers in college and seminary, we had graduated full of hopes and dreams. After all these years, to have to ask if we could stay with a family member for a few months was not easy. Mother had married Lark Villines in May of 1981 after being single for twenty-eight years. We knew Mother was love and kindness itself—Lark we didn't know well. She assured us that they both wanted us to live with them until we got back on our feet.

My grandmother was elated that we would be close by, and Frank's Dad said, "I'm glad you finally came to your senses."

Ruthie had started kindergarten in September. We knew her life would change too.

"Look, here is a picture of your grandmothers and the cousins. They are so happy that you will live nearby and they will be able to see you," I said. "Why don't you keep this picture?"

That satisfied her for the moment, and she smiled and hugged the picture to her heart. Jeanne, at the age of three years, remained happy wherever we were.

The Sunday before we left was my birthday. In the chaos of packing, I had forgotten about it; besides, money was tight. A friend had sent over a cake, that we ate with a cup of coffee, Frank handed me a small package.

"With all I'm putting you through, I couldn't let your birthday go by without doing something," he said softly, a sheepish expression on his face.

The opened package revealed a small wooden butter press. Not sure what to say, I managed a "thank you." I knew the gift was given in love, and at least it wouldn't be hard to pack. Today the memory of that butter press is as treasured as that of the dozen roses Frank gave me on my last birthday before he died.

Working according to Murphy's Law, everything that could go wrong did. We were unable to sell the Maverick or our skis, and the engine for the Comet took longer to install than Frank had planned. The day we had to load the trailer, it began snowing, plus the friend who was to keep the children fell ill. Somehow, we got packed and made arrangements with a friend to sell the car, the skis and some furniture and odds and ends. I hated to sell the baby crib that had been given to us by the church women in Kenai and felt better when we decided to give it to Friendship Mission for their church nursery.

On the last day in the apartment, I looked around the empty rooms, reminded of the homestead never settled and the log cabin house never built.

*****

Owen and Linda Fansler asked us to stay with them for our last week in Fairbanks. One evening, they sat on the sofa in their cozy living room. Frank and I sat across from them. The fire in the fireplace crackled, and the flames cast shadows on the paneled walls.

"You're so calm," Linda said.

She and Owen had worked all day, and that made us appreciate their hospitality even more.

"I guess numbness is bliss right now," I said.

"And I'm too tired from working on the car all day to feel much of anything," Frank added.

"Wish there was some way we could be of more help," Owen said.

"You are helping…"

"Having us here in your home is a great help." Frank and I tried to talk at the same time. We all fell quiet and gazed into the fire. Our close friendship spoke the love we felt for each other louder than any words.

The quiet of the moment was broken when Darcie, Ruthie, and Jeanne tottered into the room in some old high-heeled shoes. Each little girl wore a cast-off dress, and they tripped over them every step or two. Kevin clomped behind in a pair of Owen's boots and too-big blue jeans and a shirt.

"We're having a parade!" Darcie informed us. They stomped around the room a couple of times, banging on old pie tins. We clapped and cheered them on.

"A great parade," Linda said. "Now go put the clothes back in the box and wash your hands for dinner."

Ruth and Jeanne looked at me. "Yes, go on," I said.

The adults laughed. Leave it to children to balance the sober moments with joy.

How could we leave such wonderful friends?

The clock is a ruthless taskmaster, and at six o'clock in the evening on February 12, 1982, there was nothing left to say; it was time to go. I remember walking out of the Fanslers' door with tears in my eyes. I turned and said goodbye to Linda who stood at the kitchen cabinet preparing dinner.

Because the falling snow neared white-out conditions by the time we reached Delta Juncion, we spent the night in a motel. Frank had not taken time to change the oil in the car and figured he'd do that in Delta. He ran into Ray Nelson at Diehl's grocery store the next morning. Ray, a local minister who had a heated garage, told us to come on over.

"You and the girls can wait for Frank in the house. Jane is at a meeting," he told me.

"Ray, you ought to start renting out your garage," Frank joked.

"Right. Seems like you came to our rescue three years ago on New Year's Day when our Volvo broke down on the way to Cordova. Thank you," I added.

Ray laughed. "That's what friends are for."

While I waited for Frank, I remembered how Jane had fixed breakfast for us before we left for Cordova. These were the hospitable Alaskans we hated to leave.

My thoughts ran ahead to what the future might hold. Would Frank make the cut at Bein and Fushi? No way could I know then that this was not to be.

Frank interrupted my musing. "The car's ready. I'm going to wash up, then we need to get moving. Make sure the kids use the restroom before we go," he said matter-of-factly. We thanked Ray again and took off.

The road between Delta Junction and the Canadian border was bad, extremely slick with narrow shoulders. Frank was exhausted when we started, and even more so by Beaver Creek where we had to enter Canada. The Canadian border guard was a thrill a minute. Usually it was the American guards who were hard to deal with, but this guy was bad news.

He went into orbit because the travelers' checks weren't signed. In the rush of preparations, we had forgotten to sign them. The guard suspected they might be stolen. He checked Frank's drivers' license and all identification with a fine-toothed comb.

A tourist called the border patrol office while we were there. He had somehow driven past the border about fifty miles into Canada. The guard turned purple and shouted into the phone, "No one here speaks German. In plain English, you…are…in…the…coun…try il…le…gal…ly. I expect you to return to the border station, within an hour and a half."

"That poor guy. Hope he made it," Frank said as we left.

The next day, it continued snowing. We were driving over high mountains at sunset—about three o'clock—and snow whirled and blew around us.

"I can barely see the road," Frank said.

"The map shows that we should be near Summit Lodge."

We knew that one skid or wrong turn could send us careening down a mountain.

A few miles farther, he saw the sign to the lodge. "Fort Nelson's where I had hoped to spend the night. In this weather we'll never make it. Let's stop here." I didn't object.

"Not a good night to be driving. I'm glad you decided to get off the road," the friendly owner told us when we entered the lodge. "You got our last room."

After we rested and saw to the children, letting them run around a while, we joined other guests in the large dining area. A wood stove stood in one corner. What welcome warmth. Smells of beef stew and cornbread permeated the air. The middle-aged couple who owned the lodge walked among the guests, refilling water glasses and serving food. They made polite conversation with each person.

At intervals around the dining room were plaques with Bible verses. I remember reading, "Trust in the Lord with all your heart and lean not on your own understanding. In all your ways acknowledge Him and He will direct your paths" (Proverbs 3:5–6). We certainly needed to remember that.

The couple seated across from us during dinner at the lodge told us they were returning to Alaska after five years in the lower forty-eight. Frank and I looked at each other. Though their happiness at returning emphasized our sadness at leaving, we wished them well.

That night in bed, I lay awake for a while. I thought of our families in Oklahoma and Arkansas and how happy they would be to have us close by again. God would provide more Christian friends. That assurance made me rest easier.

A few days later, we drove past Dawson Creek toward Edmonton, Alberta. The landscape changed to prairie.

"I want to grab one of the receding mountains and hang on," I told Frank.

Frank gave me a knowing look. "Life goes on and we have to go with it," he said.

The words of Beryl Markham in her memoir of Africa summed up our feelings: "I knew too little of Africa [in our case, Alaska] to leave it, and what I knew, I loved too much." Discovering Alaska could take a lifetime, and we'd had only a moment.

Hidden in our hearts, though, would always be the endless treasures Alaska had given us.

I thought of our drive up the highway in 1975—the first sight of the snowcapped mountains of the north country and the promise of the rainbow over Turnagain Arm, between Anchorage and Kenai.

We were welcomed to Kenai by Bob and Ima Jean Bedwell, Glenda Kenner and the youth of the church. The Peninsula *Messiah* Chorus Frank directed had given him great joy and satisfaction.

Our pastor Don Davis and his wife Beth had encouraged and supported us that first year in Fairbanks. In 1978 we met Owen and Linda who became our closest life-long friends. And who could forget the wisdom of Ted McRoberts, the retired US Marshall, and Ethyl Peasgood, who had taught school in the bush country.

I'd learned so much by working with Valeria Sherard at Friendship Mission. The love she had for the native men, women, and children showed me how to teach with love. What blessings I would have missed had I not known her. We corresponded for many years after I left Alaska.

The seaside village of Cordova came to mind. Pastor Richard Harding and his wife, Susan, and Dick and Kay Groff had stood by us and encouraged us during a difficult time there. The pain and stress we experienced in Cordova had helped us to stand by others in their trials.

Out of the failures and disappointments faced in Alaska came the determination to get up and try again. And what is failure anyway? No failure is greater than God's power to bestow strength in the face of that weakness. Without change in our lives, we would not have known the faithfulness of God's unchanging love.

On the flyleaf of the Bible I gave Frank when he joined the air force, I wrote, "For where You go, I will go and where you lodge, I will lodge. Your people shall be my people and Your God, my God."

The words of Ruth to Naomi inspired commitment and trust in our journey together, especially in our Alaska journey. At times we wondered why we went to Alaska and if we contributed anything.

But I don't believe God wastes anything we commit to Him. In times of stress, Frank and I turned to Him for help. He led us through our maze of confusion onto solid ground.

*****

A picture of a moose standing in shallow water now hangs on my entryway wall. Though we'd never seen one until we moved to Alaska, we had several things in common with Mr. Moose. His movements were out there for everyone to see, he didn't always fit in, and hunters shot at him; still he plodded on and stood tall and proud. As a young couple serving churches in Alaska, we were closely observed. We sometimes felt like outsiders, and we were often criticized. We bravely faced trials and stood tall in the strength of the Lord.

In our first year back in the lower forty-eight, the love and support of our families helped us depend on God's strength. Edgar Hatfield, the pastor at Parkview Baptist Church in Tulsa, was also a constant encourager. He was gifted at counseling young ministers who had, as he put it, "been bruised by well-meaning church members." Eddie used some of his discretionary funds to pay Frank to assist him in calling on those who visited the church. We could never thank him enough for his friendship and compassion.

In the summer of 2014, after thirty-two years, I returned to Alaska and had the privilege of staying once more in the home of Owen and Linda. Their life journey had led them to remain in Fairbanks, while ours took us to the Southwest. On both of our journeys, we climbed the mountains that came our way. Rainbows of hope shone into each of our lives as we raised our children, worshipped, and worked. In renewing our friendship, we came to the same conclusion: it is not so important, where but *how* we live the days we are given.

I praise God that the people and places we knew in that great north country never left us—they were woven into the tapestry of our lives.

Resources

Valencia, Kris, ed. "Whitehorse." *2009 Milepost*, 182, 183
"Hal'lelu'jah"." *Peninsula Clarion* (Kenai, Alaska), March 11, 1976.
Rockwell, Kent. *Wilderness: A Journal of Quiet Adventure in Alaska*. Hanover and London: University Press of New England, 1996. 24
Cole, Terrance. "E.T. Barnette, The Strange Story of the Man Who Founded Fairbanks." *Daily News-Miner*, July 23, 1981. 14
Cole, Terrance. "E.T. Barnette, The Strange Story of the Man Who Founded Fairbanks. "*Daily News-Miner,* July 24, 1981. 7
Van Cleve, Margaret. "To the Highest Bidder!" Ruralite, October 1980. 16
Peasgood, Ethyl, and William R. Cashen. *Teaching in Alaska*. Fairbanks, AK: Alaska State Retired Teachers Association, 1976. 37
Medaris, Gene, and Ted McRoberts. *North Country Marshal*. Anchorage, AK: Great Northwest Publishing and Distributing, 1986. 26-27, 41-45, 171-173, 220
Alaska State Website. Accessed October 2015. https:///.dot.state.ak.us/amhs/community/tatitlek.
Valencia, Kris, ed. "Cordova." *2009 Milepost*, 661.
Wikipedia. Accessed November 14, 2013. https//en.wikipedia.org/miles glacier bridge.
Lowry, Robert W., ed. "How Can I Keep From Singing?" In *Bright Jewels for the Sunday School*. Bigelow and Main, 1869. hymn 16
"Beneath the Cross of Jesus." In *Baptist Hymnal*. Convention Press, 1975. 360
Browning, Robert. *Saul.* Canto XVII. New York, NY: Oxford University Press, Henry Frowde, 1909. lines 29-33

"In The Bleak Midwinter." In *United Methodist Hymnal*. United Methodist Publishing House, 1989. 221

Markham, Beryl. *West With the Night*. Boston, MA: Houghton, Mifflin and, 1942. 245

About the Author

Clyta Coder lived in Alaska from 1975 to 1982. Clyta has had articles, stories and poetry published and has written a series of Sunday school lessons for youth on the Gospel of John. Today, Clyta lives in San Antonio, Texas where she writes poetry, personal essays, and stories, serves in her church, and spends time with her two daughters and grandchildren.

CPSIA information can be obtained
at www.ICGtesting.com
Printed in the USA
FFHW020817141119
56053917-62024FF